Here's what others say about this book and the legendary Max Sackheim

"I knew, respected and learned from the renowned legend Maxwell Sackheim.

The legacy that max left for all of us in *Billion Dollar Marketing Concepts and Applications* was his timeless wisdom. A wisdom totally appropriate for the 90's.

To have Max Sackheim's recorded thoughts is to possess a treasure chest of bountiful golden nuggets."

Bob Stone
Chairman Emeritus
Stone & Adler, Inc.

"Many years ago, when I was stumbling around for a career, I had the good luck to chat with Max Sackheim in his New York office. That talk led me to the fascinating world of Direct Marketing.

Today I had more good luck. For I explored *Maxwell Sackheim's Billion Dollar Marketing Concepts and Applications*. And even now -- after I've heard it all -- I gained new insights -- and some good laughs -- from my wise old friend.

"Here is vintage Sackheim: No-frills common sense. Penetrating, pivotal insights. And straight-as-an-arrow how-to-do-it advice.

Freshman, sophomores and seniors in every branch of the ad business have much to learn from Max Sackheim. And if you are a beginner, he might even change your life -- as he did mine. Thanks again, Max!"

Sig Rosenblum
Sig Rosenblum, Inc.

"Maxwell Sackheim beat new and enduring paths into the wilderness of communications. He was a great pioneer."

William Bernbach
Doyle, Dane, Bernbach

"I picked up several useful tips I can immediately use from *Maxwell Sackheim's Billion Dollar Marketing Concepts and Applications*.

Anyone who seriously wants to improve their direct response results should buy this book."

Ted Nicholas, Author
How To Form Your Own Corporation Without A Lawyer For Under $75, and Direct Marketing Success Letter.

"MAIL ORDER EXECUTIVES will revel reading *Maxwell Sackheim's Billion Dollar Marketing Concepts and Applications*. His legendary advertising agency created many of America's top mail order campaigns in space and direct mail."

Pete Hoke
Hoke Communications, Inc.

"The name Maxwell Sackheim is synonymous with outstanding results in direct mail advertising. Since the Sackheim legend is true, his place as the 'dean of direct mail' is secure in the history of marketing communications."

Ed Acree
Wilson & Acres

"I have learned a lot from Maxwell Sackheim."
David Ogilvy
Olgilvy & Mather

"For sheer sales power and barehanded accomplishment, Max Sackheim stands alone!"
Rosser Reeves
Former Chairman of Ted Bates

Maxwell Sackheim's

Billion Dollar Marketing

CONCEPTS AND APPLICATIONS

The Man Who
Revolutionized 20th Century
Direct Response Advertising

Compiled by Jerry Major Buchanan and David A. Reecher

TOWERS CLUB USA PRESS • VANCOUVER, WASHINGTON

BILLION DOLLAR MARKETING
CONCEPTS AND APPLICATIONS

By Maxwell Sackheim
The Man Who Revolutionized 20th Century
Direct Response Advertising

Published by:
TOWERS Club, USA Press
Post Office Box 2038
Vancouver, WA 98668-2038 U.S.A.

Cover Design by
Foster & Foster, Inc.
104 South 2nd St., Fairfield, IA 52556
(800) 472-3953

Library of Congress Catalog Card Number: 95-60017
ISBN: 0-930668-11-1 Softcover

PRINTED IN THE UNITED STATES OF AMERICA

ACKNOWLEDGMENTS

We would like to thank a few special people who helped make this a great book!

First, Robert & Sherman Sackheim, the sons of the late Maxwell Sackheim, who supported us in many ways during the publication of this book. In addition to their moral support, they also provided many of the great speeches, articles, and ads used in book two. To them, we owe our deep appreciation.

Andi Emerson, a dear friend of Max's, for her many insights and overall suggestions used.

To Don Crissey and his personal library, for providing many of the hard-to-find magazine ads.

To George Foster (Foster & Foster, Fairfield, IA) for creating such a great cover design, and for all the additional help that he provided.

Patsy Conner and Cheryl Reecher, for all their hard work and dedication during the proofreading and editing stages of this book.

When this book was almost complete and ready to go to press, we sent galley's to some of Max's friends and colleagues. We would like to give a special thanks to *Bob Stone, Sig Rosenblum, Ted Nicholas,* and *Pete Hoke,* whose comments arrived before press time and are printed on page one.

TABLE OF CONTENTS

ILLUSTRATIONS

Maxwell Sackheim — *The Legend Continues*

If you are one of the few people who has never heard of the man Maxwell B. Sackheim, you are in for one of the greatest "reads" of your life. These three individual books may be small, but that's because Max didn't require volumes of print to deliver his pearls of advertising wisdom. Great copywriters always seem to be born with the innate ability to exemplify that great quote attributed to Sydney Smith, (1771-1845): "The writer does the most who gives his reader the most knowledge and takes from him the least time." Max was one of the greatest copywriters and creative thinkers of all time. Although he sold hundreds of different products and services during his career, probably the greatest thing he ever sold was his uncommon wisdom in each of several books he authored. Max had a way of looking through the cumbersome details of any given project and seeing only the plain simple logic needed to reach customers in the greatest numbers at the least expense to his clients, and to make them want to buy. Toward the close of his active Madison Avenue career, and after he had retired to Florida, Max started a second career as a successful author. His books "My First 65 years In Advertising", "The Seven Deadly Sins" series (of three books), and "How To Advertise Yourself" are collector's items now and anyone who owns one or more of these would never think of loaning them out. Now this book, which may be the greatest of all, is his last gift to an admiring public. His very uncommon "common sense" will delight you on every page.

During the last decade of his life, Max and I became friendly correspondents, he in his Florida home and I in my Vancouver, Washington one. I grew to love this gentleman and consider it one of the greatest compliments of my life that he in turn admired me as a warm human being and a fair country copywriter too. But it wasn't until 1978 that we got a chance to meet in person. He and his wife, Mary, had flown out to the Northwest for Mary's high school reunion. While here, I had the privilege of their company for a full afternoon in my home. Nattily dressed in a summer-blue suit and a red necktie, Max was a picture to behold. But perhaps the most notable aspect of his physical appearance was his height. He couldn't have been over five feet tall. But one had only to listen to him talk for five minutes to recognize that he was a true giant. He loved his country and he loved his God. He loved humanity and he loved the advertising game.

The great French poet and novelist Victor Hugo once observed: "There is no such thing as a little country. The greatness of a people is no more determined by their number than the greatness of a man is determined by his height." I never fail to think of my friend and colleague, Maxwell B. Sackheim every time I run across that quote. This man, with only a sixth grade formal education to his credit academically, is one of the shining and bright human tributes to a country that allows any person to make of themselves what they will.

Max passed over on December 2nd, 1982 at the age of 92. He is survived by his two sons, Sherman and Robert.

There are only a handful of truly great men born to each century. Max Sackheim was one of those for the Twentieth Century. May you profit in many ways from this legacy in print. We won't see his likes again in this lifetime.

— Jerry Buchanan

PREFACE

MAXWELL B. SACKHEIM
Born: September 25, 1890
Died: December 2, 1982

When we decided to publish Max Sackheim's last recorded thoughts and words in this book, we started with the original manuscript Max had sent me before his death on December 2nd 1982. His suggested title was "How To Sell Anything By Mail". But as we dug deeper and deeper into the Max Sackheim story, and talked with his two living sons, Sherman and Robert, we came up with so much other fascinating material by and about Max that we felt we had to change the title and add two other books under the same cover.

BOOK ONE   We call the first book Maxwell Sackheim on Direct Response Marketing in which he gives the reader far more than just how to sell anything by mail. He delves deeply into the subtle shadings of psychology necessary to make the buying public respond with money if the offer is right. He dissects the art of selling and lays the microscopic filets of data before us as no other advertising genius has ever done. In Book One, Max does not just give the readers a few "fish from his creel". That would only feed them for a day or two. Instead, he teaches them how to fish for the prize catches and feed themselves for a lifetime. Many of the most famous names in modern-day advertising regard Max Sackheim as "The Man Who Revolutionized 20th Century Advertising". His unique concepts stand alone in the annals of the field and are the most oft copied of this or any other century. Who among us hasn't heard of the "Book-of-the-Month-Club" or the "Negative Option Plan?" Those are only two of Max Sackheim's many original unique selling propositions. Both proved "Pure Mother Lode" to every company that ever adapted them to their own sales campaigns. And Max never received a penny in royalty rights for them. They became public domain. Now they also become yours for having purchased this last legacy from "The Little Giant of 20th Century Advertising". (Max Sackheim stood 5'-2" and only completed the sixth grade of elementary school — but his original marketing ideas were Herculean!)

BOOK TWO was added between these covers because we came across a wealth of other materials. Here are speeches, articles and essays written by the man, and several display ads he or his advertising agency created from 1916 through the '20s, '30s, '40s, and '50s.

His ads for the "Little Leather Library" are fascinating for their simplicity and for how they so clearly demonstrate the AICDA formula (action, interest, confidence, desire, action) and Max's system of "building buyer lists" with break-even or loss-leader offers. (i.e. "30 Classic Volumes for $2.98 ppd").

BOOK THREE   The History of Advertising could have been published under a separate cover as another literary product. Max loved the field of advertising so much that in his spare time, when he wasn't burning his mental molecules for clients, he was researching the field of advertising. He had an insatiable curiosity about how and when man first thought of publicly announcing his wants, needs and services (advertising) to a wide variety of potential customers. What Max found in his research effort makes Book Three a fascinating read all by itself.

With all due respect for the other handful of great advertising brains of the twentieth century, we humbly present this anthology and tribute to Maxwell B. Sackheim — a unique entity and a giant in his own right.

The compilers,
Jerry Buchanan, President & CEO
David A. Reecher, Associate Director
TOWERS Club Press, Inc.
Post Office Box 2038
Vancouver, WA 98668-2038

Billion Dollar Marketing
CONCEPTS AND APPLICATIONS

BOOK ONE

Maxwell Sackheim

on Direct Response

Marketing

CHAPTER ONE

DIRECT RESPONSE SELLING

Some of the top men in mail order were greatly concerned.

As far as I can trace it, selling by mail on a commercial scale was started in 1870 by a gentleman named A. Montgomery Ward. Messrs. Sears and Roebuck followed. Most sales were made to farmers who lived far from town, and in those days, any distance was far from town. I'm not as old as Ward or Sears, but I remember when farmers had to go to the nearest post office to pick up their letters and packages. The trip was only made once a week because the roads were terrible, and their only means of transportation was the old horse and buggy. When automobiles and good roads came into being, it became very easy to get to town. Some of the top men in the mail order business were greatly concerned because it seemed there would be no more need for shopping by mail. Their customers could get to town in minutes every day instead of in hours only once a week. Shopping was made easier because the customer could actually see, touch, and sample the items before they made the purchase. Decisions could be made on the spot instead of having to send hundreds of miles for the order - waiting days or even weeks for the purchase to arrive. Then, if it was the wrong size, color, or whatever, it would have to be returned, causing further delay.

In spite of automobiles, telephones, movies, chain stores, supermarkets, enormous retail outlets and the demands of radio and television, the mail order business has become even greater than it was in the horse and buggy days.

Sears and Wards do more business by mail now than they did when buying by mail was almost a necessity. And not only is it true of Wards and Sears, but of thousands of other large and small enterprises which deal almost entirely by mail. And why not?

Buying by mail is economical, convenient and safe; it avoids the crush of crowds, eliminates parking problems and enables new enterprises to start small without long term obligations.

By the time he got through, that piano wasn't playing anything but sour music.

When I was working for Sears, I heard of a conspiracy entered into by the merchants in certain towns. They ordered and paid for many hundreds of dollars worth of merchandise only to return the unopened boxes and crates to Sears or Wards for a refund. The purpose, of course, was to discourage Sears and Wards from sending catalogs to those towns. Another story concerned a local piano dealer who was called in to tune a piano purchased from Sears. By the time he got through, that piano wasn't playing anything but sour music. In self defense or in desperation, Sears sent a man there. Not only did he tune the piano properly but actually ripped it apart to prove to the purchaser that the wood was as represented and the value greater than its price would purchase locally. When the public discovered how generous Sears was in making adjustments and refunds, they began to believe more and more in mail order marketing as a method of saving time and money.

Mail order, or as many today prefer to call it, Direct Response Marketing, is not confined to the sale of merchandise. It can, should be, and is used to increase store traffic, get more leads for salespeople, build good will, get ideas from customers, bring former customers back, increase memberships, raise funds for worthy causes, broaden lines, win the favor of sources of supply, cut down overhead -- and for many other business-building purposes.

Does the merchandise or service offered justify a purchase "sight-unseen" by mail?

There has never been a time, as far back as I can remember, when obstacles and hurdles were not placed in the path of mail marketing activities. Today, as always, anyone engaged in direct marketing must be greatly concerned with the answer to several vital problems, upon the solution of which success or failure depends. These are: Does the merchandise or service offered justify a purchase "sight-unseen" by mail? Is it exclusive or is it easily obtained in any corner store? Is it offered at a worthwhile savings? Is it something that can be mailed for a small percentage of its total price? The ideal item, as I have often said, is a diamond and the worst an anvil. Is the margin of profit, not merely percentage-wise, but unit-wise, large enough to cover all costs plus a net profit? Is it something that lends itself to repeat sales of the same or other related items thus creating a long time customer instead of merely a one-time sale? Is it something that will indicate to others in direct marketing that your list of customers could be extremely valuable to them? Is it something that is independent of size, color, mechanical skill or other factors mainly responsible for returns, exchanges or repairs? Is it something that will make your customers happy, not only to have purchased for themselves but to purchase as gifts for others, and that will justify them in recommending you to their friends? Is it something you would be happy to live with?

No business is easy and the mail order business demands more than most in imagination and strategy. You can't hope to be successful in it if you think on a part-time basis. Your product and method of distributing it deserves the limit of your financial backing and you should spend at least eight hours a day thinking about it.

First you must have a good product.

See Little Leather Library ads on pages 53-54 for examples of buying customers quickly.

Second, you must be adequately capitalized so you can afford to **buy customers** instead of expecting to make a profit on every initial sale.

Third, you can't afford to dilly-dally in building up a list of customers. If your pace is too slow, your overhead will devour you. This may be no different from other methods of doing business, but in selling by mail you can do a lot to control the speed of obtaining new customers.

Fourth, you must continually go after repeat orders and multiple sales. This will give you the necessary capital for acquiring new customers.

Fifth, you must be on the alert to expand operations and lengthen the selling and buying season.

In short, you must use as much mail order and business experience as can be digested whether it comes from Sears, Montgomery Ward, Book-of-the-Month-Club, competitors, or from some of the thousands of failures that may warn you away from dangers.

You can't find a better salesman.

Use direct response advertising carefully and wisely. You can't find a better potential salesman. He won't get drunk. He won't get sick. He won't misrepresent you. He will work 24 hours a day, 7 days a week, 52 weeks a year. He will tell your story as well as **you** tell it.

Put mail order on your payroll at so much a week or a month.

You can tailor your campaign to your purse. You can reach 100, 1,000, 5,000 or hundreds of thousands of people. If you have a business that is making money with other methods of distribution, put mail order on your payroll at so much a week or a month, or a year, just as you would employ a new salesman who has made a reputation in some other line or with some other company. You would give him a chance to make good even if you lost money on him for a while.

Rich or poor, we have holes in our pockets burned there by money that wants to be exchanged for whatever else we desire more.

There is no easy road to success in the mail order business, but when you discover the right formula you can travel safely and swiftly to your desired goal. Selling is merely a matter of justifying buying. Rich or poor, we have holes in our pockets burned there by money that wants to be exchanged for whatever else we desire more. Sometimes we even spend money we don't have -- mortgaging our future earnings for the things we want now.

SHOULD I GO INTO THE MAIL ORDER BUSINESS?

By all means -- if you want to go into a business and **not an easy business.** If you want to get rich quick, if you want a one shot deal, if you don't think you could succeed in any business, stay out of the mail order business. If you haven't sufficient capital -- and

I mean twice as much as you **think** you need -- stay out. If you have another business to which you can add a mail order department or if your merchandise or service lends itself to mail order selling -- and if you can meet all the other qualifications that make a businessman successful, fine. You'll get a big kick out of mail order operating, and maybe you'll even make a profit.

WHEN ARE CONDITIONS FAVORABLE TO START A MAIL ORDER BUSINESS?

It's a great deal tougher when you have to start from scratch. You have to find space, build an organization, hire help and do everything from the ground up. But, if you have a going business and can siphon off some of the profits for experimental work in mail order, the headaches are less. You're working out of a basic business. You have a good start. You're moving but perhaps tackling it from another direction. It's better to add a business to another business than to begin from a standing position -- just like adding a new item to a line.

WHAT IS THE MOST IMPORTANT FACTOR IN A DIRECT MAIL EFFORT?

What you are offering is the most important factor. And what you are offering may be a new idea, a new result, a new price, a new guarantee, or a new service.

This can very easily make or break your efforts regardless of what's inside.

As to the most important detail, I think your outside envelope is terribly important. It should carry the headline of your ad. This can very easily make or break your efforts regardless of what's inside. Don't tell so much on the envelope that the reader "knows" he doesn't want what you're offering inside. Don't be so smart, so clever, or so unbelievable as a result of whatever you print on the envelope that the recipient subconsciously says "nuts," "baloney" or worse, "more junk mail". If you can't say anything on the outside of the envelope that will be of genuine interest to the reader, say nothing.

WHAT IS A PRIME REQUISITE FOR A "BREAK" IN THE MAIL ORDER BUSINESS?

You make your own "breaks". One must be a good business person before one can become a success in the mail order business. You must be able to plan and project. You must learn how to buy, to organize, to finance and to expand rapidly if the responses come in fast. To my mind, management is as important as the merchandise and the advertising. Too many good items and good ads smash on the rocks because of bad management.

WHAT IS THE CRITERIA OF A SUCCESSFUL MAIL ORDER THEME?

That's why the "inertia plan" in club operations is so successful. (Negative Option Plan)

Some of us fail to realize that **in business** you must aim to **buy a customer** -- not merely make a sale. The original order is vitally important but you haven't a business unless it includes some habit or repeat characteristic. That's one reason why magazines can afford to lose money on a trial subscription -- that's why the "inertia plan" in club operations is so successful -- it keeps the item going out "til forbid". Of course, this method of selling requires courage, capital and above all QUALITY and VALUE! In buying a sale, you must be able to last it out and project the customer into a buying habit pattern.

ARE THERE ANY ADVANTAGES?

Your market is limited to about 50 million families.

To paraphrase an old expression "there's no business like the mail order business" -- stop and think of its many advantages. You don't have to wait for business to come to you. You go after it. You can deal with people anywhere. Your market is limited to about 50 million families. There's no parking problem. There's no problem of meeting customers face to face. It's the best way yet discovered to decentralize. It doesn't make much difference where you are located. And best of all, it's bigger now than ever before and still growing rapidly as we head into the 21st Century!

Anything to remove resistance to buying.

Anything to prove your merchandise can stand the test of inspection.

Today's facilities for reproducing products, sampling products and the fact that so many companies sell merchandise by mail that is also sold over the counter, would indicate that there is a buyer's universe other than shoppers in the malls. Transportation is getting more difficult, shopping centers are more crowded, road traffic more congested, parking more scarce and competition more and more severe among merchants themselves. So if you're not greedy, you can do a fine job by mail. Of course, you have to use the same methods that have already been successful. Sampling, time payment, and if you can afford it, "on approval" merchandise is important. Anything to remove resistance to buying. Anything to prove your merchandise can stand the test of inspection.

In the coming years, the present volume will seem small. It's the easiest way to buy -- and the easiest way to sell! All we have to do is give our customers good value and good treatment, and we'll build greater confidence and greater sales every year. Even if postage rates and all other costs continue to go up, we'll continue to survive.

As for products of the future that will be sold by direct mail, one has to be pretty much of a fortune teller. But I think there's no reason in the world why the merchandise sold in the stores should not be sold by mail. There's an old axiom in mail order: "the higher the price, the lighter the weight, the bigger the margin of profit, the better the item is for mail order selling." That's because transportation charges are a constant and relative cost factor as is the cost of getting a customer in relation to the value of the product. The repeat value of merchandise is also a tremendous factor. So all these things have to be taken into consideration when you're marketing a product by mail.

*P*eople go through life with their minds only half turned on, except when they're promised an adequate reward for their full attention. Ordinarily their attitude toward nearly everything they see, read, hear and experience is "SO WHAT?".

-- Maxwell B. Sackheim

CHAPTER TWO

WRITING COPY

WRITING COPY

If you believe in a proposition, you're a much better writer than if you're only an advertising person.

The basic difference between an average direct mail ad-writer and an extraordinary one is frequently only the absolute sincerity in writing. If you believe in a proposition -- firmly believe in it -- you're a much better writer than if you're only an advertising person. In fact, poor writers can do better than good writers if they're more sincere about what they're writing. If I were a good prospect I could do a good job myself of writing to tell others, and if I didn't believe in the product I'd be a poor prospect. If you can't sell yourself, you can't sell anybody else and all you become is a hypocritical liar by trying to do so.

Writers or specialty salespersons can try to force enthusiasm about anything handed them to sell. But if they really don't believe in it or like it, they're forced to manufacture insincere rhetoric. **Persons of integrity** can't deliver convincing copy about a product or service unless they're sold on it themselves.

If it appeals to your own good taste, you'll have no problem selling its merits to others. Your ad copy will just seem to flow effortlessly.

In it he advanced four cardinal rules of successful copy.

I always come back to the formula advanced many years ago by Walter Dill Scott of Northwestern University. He was then Professor of Psychology and later became President of the University. He wasn't even an advertising man, but he wrote a book in 1906 entitled **"The Psychology of Advertising"**. In it he advanced four cardinal rules of successful copy. These are still valid. At least I've never seen, heard or read better ones despite the new jargon about motivation, research, depth interviews and the like. These four requisites are ATTRACTION, INTEREST, CONVICTION and ACTION.

Give the reader a chance to make a deal with you--not tomorrow or next week but RIGHT AWAY.

Advertising is wasteful if it doesn't get action. One response may be worth a thousand impressions. If after attracting, interesting and convincing a prospect you fail to get an order, an inquiry, a phone call, a personal call or whatever responses you want, you've shot a lot of ammunition into the air without bringing down a dollar. Give the reader a chance to make a deal with you -- not tomorrow or next week but RIGHT AWAY. Leaving him to dangle in no man's land is an opportunity lost.

DIRECT MAIL

You can simply write a letter that makes a unique offer.

Direct mail has an advantage over periodical advertising. In direct mail you don't have to worry about the competitive ads on the other pages. You can simply write a letter that makes a unique offer. All you have to do is get the right merchandise at the right price, and present it honestly and plainly to your prospective buyers.

One of the troubles with in-print magazine advertising today is that too many people are trying to be clever.

One of the troubles with in-print magazine advertising today is that too many people are trying to be clever. They are doing things which destroy the desire to read and believe the ads. Even art directors are making it difficult for people to read ads. It is difficult enough to convince people, but when you get headlines and pictures unrelated to the product being offered or backgrounds that make it hard to read the type, the difficulty of making a sale is even greater.

When you begin to exaggerate, today's buyers shut you off immediately.

A proposition makes the advertising man, the advertising man does not make the proposition. I think honesty is one of the greatest factors you can possibly use in the sale of merchandise today, and one of the best examples of that is the advertising of the Volkswagen. When they came out and said this is the ugliest car made but the cheapest to run, they did everything they possibly could to convince you they were telling the truth about their product. The public has confidence when you tell the truth. When you begin to exaggerate, today's buyers shut you off immediately. They have become far more sophisticated in detecting phony advertising messages than they were years ago. So if you want to sell, tell the truth!

Ordinarily their attitude toward nearly everything they see, read, hear and experience is "so what?".

How can we make the best use of this wonderful, convenient, economic tool of communication? We must realize that our customers are equipped with built in clickers which enable them to automatically shut out practically anything they don't want to hear or see -- including advertising. People go through life with their minds only half turned on, except when they're promised an adequate reward for their full attention. Ordinarily their attitude toward nearly everything they see, read, hear and experience is "So what?". They hate to bother changing their minds, their habits, or their routines.

There are four "why's" to be remembered and answered in each copywriting job you undertake.

(1)   **Why should anyone read or listen to it?**
(2)   **Why should anyone believe it?**
(3)   **Why should anyone do anything about it?**
(4)   **Why should it be acted upon immediately?**

Make it easier to say yes than to say no.

When you write your copy in such a way that those four "why's" get a good believable and solid "because", you have written a world-beating ad. Properly worded, the ad and the offer make it easier for the prospect to say "YES" than to say "NO". By anticipating all possible objections and answering them, the copywriter has closed all the corral gates except one, and that one remaining open gate is the one that leads the prospect into the buyer's chute.

If you don't get them into your "store" how are you going to sell 'em?

To induce people to drop everything in order to pay attention to you, you must shock, startle, promise a worthwhile reward, or in some other way shake them out of their inattention. You can't expect them to read your story unless it's more important than whatever it is they are doing or thinking about at the moment. If you don't get their attention, how are you going to get 'em into your store? And if you don't get 'em into your "store", how are you going to sell 'em?

So first analyze the product. Think of it in terms of it being a patent medicine. What symptoms does it relieve? Bear in mind that nothing is bought unless there's some reason for buying it. That reason is the symptom that exists **or which you must create.** It may be boredom, loneliness, hunger, thirst, ambition, greed, the desire for popularity, security, entertainment, or affection. All these are symptoms and there are many, many others.

We must take the ordinary items and create some news about them.

When you think about it, nearly all products are just ordinary. There are very few new and desirable inventions or ideas that can be sold by mail. There are only a few "red hot" items and we can't wait for them to come our way. So we must take the ordinary items and create some news about them.

It wasn't too long ago the only way to consume oranges and tomatoes was to eat them. Now we drink orange juice, tomato juice, prune juice and cranberry juice. Flowers are now messages since "Say it with flowers" became part of our national vernacular. Perhaps the most important NEWS about your product might be price, or terms, or a guarantee. It may be the result or benefit the product provides, or it may be the product itself! Search and discover the hidden values in your product. Draw on that from a newsy angle; glamorize it. Perhaps it may help if you think in terms of headlines. When you get a "so what?" reaction, it's no good.

Never think of your prospect as a mailing list or a statistic.

Analyze your prospect; their age, sex, likes and dislikes. What other products might they be interested in buying from you? Think of one such person -- a person you may even know -- and appeal to that person. Never think of your prospect as a mailing list or a statistic. Think of that person as though you were going to talk to him individually. And contrary to some beliefs, most people like to get letters.

I remember one book called **"Power of Will"** written by a fellow named Frank Channing Haddock. The book explained how to use your will power to get what you want. It was very difficult to understand and very difficult to read. However, prior to that a famous professor at Harvard, (and probably the first popular, great American psychologist) William James, wrote a book on psychology and it included a chapter on will power. If you read his book and then wrote the ad for Haddock's book, you had a good ad. The **"Power of Will"** was offered on an approval basis, and if not acceptable could be sent back. The title, more than the actual content, sold the book and people were reluctant to send it back because doing so showed weak will power, the very thing the book schooled the reader against.

"Power of Will" ad featured on next page.

Regardless of what you promise, if your readers do not believe it you are sunk. We have all read the silliest reasons for hurrying up. We can't bring ourselves to believe the reason why certain offers must end in 10 days. We know of time-limit offers that were phony because they sounded funny. This also applies to special prices, to free deals, etc. Your sincerity may be questioned by your language or by the appearance of your mailing. "To thine own self be true" as the poet says, "and it follows as night the day thou can'st not then be false to any man".

You have to do it on the basis of creating good will!

You have to be honest in your advertising. That's the first thing, because if you don't create satisfied customers who recommend you to other prospects, you'll never succeed in the mail order business. You can't do it on a one-time sale or a two-time sale. You have to do it on the basis of creating good will! Customers are your best prospects! Get customers no matter what it costs.

You can get a return on your investment every time you roll out with a new project.

If your merchandise and offer is good and your profit margin is adequate, you can get a return on your investment every time you roll out with a new project.

The public is the final judge of what is being offered, and any failure to capture the public's imagination may be due to the fact that you didn't use enough of your own!

To sustain interest, give your prospect news. Yes, news interests people. Are you giving your prospects all the newest news about your product or are you taking too much for granted? As Elmer Wheeler said, "Sell the sizzle, not the steak".

Don't underestimate the intelligence of the average reader.

If you're not a Christian Scientist, it would be difficult to sell Christian Science to others. If you're not a Catholic, it might be difficult to sell Catholicism to somebody who isn't, and the same would be true of any religion. Conviction depends upon believability. No matter what you say, if it isn't believed, you've lost your sale. Believability is born of sincerity. Don't underestimate the intelligence of the average reader. You know when you are stretching the truth beyond reason, and so does your prospect. Even if you succeed in selling by overselling, you may be losing a customer -- and the success or failure of your business depends upon the number of customers you make, not the number of sales. Remember this: Even an uneducated person's reading vocabulary is much greater than his speaking vocabulary. So don't talk down to your prospect.

If you are making a time limit offer give a reason for it --a good reason.

If you are testing a price, why not say you don't know whether or not you can continue -- it will all depend upon how many you sell. If you are making a time limit offer give a reason for it -- a good reason. And **have** a good reason! Never underestimate the intelligence of the public.

SOME BASIC RULES FOR WRITING
MAIL ORDER COPY:

It must be thorough - nothing must be left to the reader's imagination.

It must be credible - no one buys an obvious untruth.

It must be sincere - insincerity unsells.

It must be a bargain in one form or another.

It must be a bargain in one form or another - in health, knowledge, goods -- worthy of an exchange for money; worthy of the effort involved in buying by mail.

It must be made attractive enough to justify stopping - reading - believing and ACTING.

**If your product and your offer are right,
your copy almost writes itself.**

You can't determine the acceptability of a product, but I do think nearly every product has many possible appeals and every appeal may change the product itself.

These are but a few examples of how important it may be to make your product different.

For many years Listerine was used chiefly for the relief of sore throats, then someone made an entirely new product out of it by offering it as a remedy for halitosis. A new commodity was created when books began to be sold on a club membership basis. Noxzema is now a beauty cream instead of only a sunburn reliever. Even automobiles are not merely transportation. During the Second World War we learned that a car could be driven for ten years or longer, but they've made us style and color conscious. Insurance isn't death insurance, it is life insurance. These are but a few examples of how important it may be to make your product different from what it is now even if it isn't changed a bit.

The way to find this new product within the old one is to analyze every possible consumer symptom. Ask yourself **"What do people want?"**.

Don't sell the product, sell the benefit it will create

The old patent medicine hawkers used to claim a cure for everything from fallen arches to falling hair; from backaches to toothaches to bellyaches to earaches. Even today the old techniques for selling patent medicines work when you think about it. All you have to do is look for the most universal symptoms your product will "cure", **or create a symptom.** I'm sure if you hit the right one, your copy writing job will be a lot easier. You won't have to struggle so hard with words. You won't even have to scramble for clever approaches or word combinations. Your basic idea will attract interest. **Don't sell the product, sell the benefit it will create!** You can beat your brains out trying to say new things about the same old product -- so you must apply new and radical thinking to your product. Make a new product out of it.

HOW LONG SHOULD A SALES LETTER BE?

The length of the letter in inches or pages is not what determines its readership.

Are your letters long enough, or too long? Listen! Any letter that is **uninteresting** is too long. Even a short letter can be too long if it's boring! The length of the letter in inches or pages is not what determines its readership. Even busy executives read everything that interests them. This has been proven so many times I won't elaborate further except to say the secret of gaining and retaining the interest of a prospective customer is to transform yourself into a prospect. Write yourself the kind of letter you would like to get. Begin where the customer's thoughts are -- on himself, his family, his home, his problems, his hopes and his desires. Too many direct mail letters say "I want to sell you" instead of "I want to serve you".

The writer should have gone for the close just before that question came up.

Frankly I prefer short letters -- the shorter the better. I consider my time my most valuable possession. And yet, if it takes several pages for me to get the complete story, **after you have captured my full interest and attention and desire to continue reading**, that letter is not too long! People who say they seldom read long letters are right, except that length depends upon holding interest. If your letter is interesting, don't worry about the number of words or pages. Only when the reader's attention begins to lag and the letter ceases to hold their interest has it finally gone on too long. When it begins to ask "Am I boring you?" you know the answer is automatically "Yes". The writer should have gone for the close just before that question came up.

SHOULD A LETTER BE BROKEN WITH SUBHEADS?

Even the most sophisticated of us read form letters - provided they are about things in which we have some interest.

Yes -- if your subheads can be made to mean something. If used merely for the purpose of breaking up the monotony of the page, they may drive the reader away. They should be enticing, promising, and rewarding. The same is true of the use of a second color in a letter. If carelessly done the second color may actually induce skipping, but if tied in as part of a paragraph instead of a whole paragraph, if used to make subheads stand out, I am sure they induce reading. We must remember that people like to receive mail. They read form letters avidly if they are interested. Even the most sophisticated of us read form letters whether Hooverized, offset, lithographed, letterpress or imitation hand written -- provided they are about things in which we have some interest. Don't for one moment think third class mail is thrown away without getting a chance to claim attention.

WHAT ABOUT ILLUSTRATED LETTERS?

Try to make the illustrations mean something. If they are good copy, they are good. If they are used simply to brighten up a page the illustration loses its value. If not properly used, it may add to the "add-i-ness" of your letter, making it a circular instead of a letter. I feel a letter should be a letter, and a circular should be a circular. Unless you can combine the two in an inconspicuous way, keep them separate.

HOW DO YOU DECIDE UPON THE GENERAL TONE OF A SALES LETTER?

The product generally selects the audience.

It seems to me the general tone of your letter should be determined by two things: (a) the product you are selling, and (b) the type of prospect. They can be a hillbilly or an executive, and if you are selling ukeleles, your language can be the same to all. If you are selling a financial service or a fine magazine, your prospects may be lawyers, doctors, clergymen, bakers, butchers, or candlestick makers -- the product generally selects the audience. I do not believe in bribing the reader into reading anything not legitimate to his means or his needs. Know your product -- and your prospect. Your language will take care of itself.

Do You Make These Mistakes In English?

Ad featured on next page.

The best ad I ever wrote was written in 1918 for the Sherwin Cody School of English. Its headline was "Do You Make These Mistakes In English?". It just happened to be timely and it happened to be written to myself. I was the guy who wanted to become a master of English. Old Sherwin Cody, himself, would come in to see me time after time about the ad and point out mistakes in English, and it impressed me very much. Each time we had to change the ad. Even after the ad was placed and running, somebody would point out more mistakes in English, so we had to make more changes. The original ad was written very quickly, possibly a couple of days, but the changes were made over a period of time.

That ad was one determining factor in putting my name in the all-time Copywriter's Hall of Fame. It didn't run too often and not in too many publications, but it ran for over 40 years. Other copywriters compared its results with a lot of other ads but "Do You Make These Mistakes In English" always came out the best.

Do You Make These Mistakes in English?

Sherwin Cody's remarkable invention has enabled more than 100,000 people to correct their mistakes in English. Only 15 minutes a day required to improve your speech and writing.

MANY persons use such expressions as "Leave them lay there" and "Mary was invited as well as myself." Still others say "between you and I" instead of "between you and me." It is astonishing how often "who" is used for "whom" and how frequently we hear such glaring mispronunciations as "for MID able," "ave NOO," and "KEW pon." Few know whether to spell certain words with one or two "c's" or "m's" or "r's" or with "ie" or "ei," and when to use commas in order to make their meaning absolutely clear. Most persons use only common words—colorless, flat, ordinary. Their speech and their letters are lifeless, monotonous, humdrum.

Why Most People Make Mistakes

What is the reason so many of us are deficient in the use of English and find our careers stunted in consequence? Why is it some cannot spell correctly and others cannot punctuate? Why do so many find themselves at a loss for words to express their meaning adequately? The reason for the deficiency is clear. Sherwin Cody discovered it in scientific tests which he gave thousands of times. *Most persons do not write or speak good English simply because they never formed the habit of doing so.*

What Cody Did at Gary

The formation of any habit comes only from constant practice. Shakespeare, you may be sure, never studied rules. No one who writes and speaks correctly thinks of *rules* when he is doing so.

Here is our mother-tongue, a language that has built up our civilization, and without which we should all still be muttering savages! Yet our schools, by wrong methods, have made it a study to be avoided—the hardest of tasks instead of the most fascinating of games! For years it has been a crying disgrace.

In that point lies the real difference between Sherwin Cody and the schools! Here is an illustration: Some years ago Mr. Cody was invited by the author of the famous Gary System of Education to teach

SHERWIN CODY

English to all upper-grade pupils in Gary, Indiana. By means of unique practice exercises *Mr. Cody secured more improvement in these pupils in five weeks than previously had been obtained by similar pupils in two years under old methods.* There was no guesswork about these results. They wer proved by scientific comparisons. Amazing as this improvement was, more interesting still was the fact that the children were "wild" about the study. It was like playing a game!

The basic principle of Mr. Cody's new method is habit-forming. Anyone can learn to write and speak correctly by constantly using the correct forms. But how is one to know in each case what is correct? Mr. Cody solves this problem in a simple, unique, sensible way.

100% Self-Correcting Device

Suppose he himself were standing forever at your elbow. Every time you mispronounced or misspelled a word, every time you violated correct grammatical usage, every time you used the wrong word to express what you meant, suppose you could hear him whisper: "That is wrong, it should be thus and so." In a short time you would habitually use the correct form and the right words in speaking and writing.

If you continued to make the same mistakes over and over again, each time patiently he would tell you what was right. He would, as it were, be an everlasting mentor beside you—a mentor who would not laugh at you, but who would, on the contrary, support and help you. The 100% Self-Correcting Device does exactly this thing. It is Mr. Cody's silent voice behind you, ready to speak out whenever you commit an error. It finds your mistakes and concentrates on them. You do not need to study anything you already know. There are no rules to memorize.

Only 15 Minutes a Day

Nor is there very much to learn. In Mr. Cody's years of experimenting he brought to light some highly astonishing facts about English.

For instance, statistics show that a list of sixty-nine words (with their repetitions) *make up more than half of all our speech and letter-writing.* Obviously, if one could learn to spell, use, and pronounce these words correctly, one would go far toward eliminating incorrect spelling and pronunciation.

Similarly, Mr. Cody proved that there were no more than one dozen fundamental principles of punctuation. If we mastered these principles, there would be no bugbear of punctuation to handicap us in our writing.

Finally he discovered that twenty-five typical errors in grammar constitute nine-tenths of our everyday mistakes. When one has learned to avoid these twenty-five pitfalls, how readily one can obtain the facility of speech which denotes the person of breeding and education!

When the study of English is made so simple, it becomes clear that progress can be made in a very short time. *No more than fifteen minutes a day is required.* Fifteen minutes, not of study, but of fascinating practice! Mr. Cody's students do their work in any spare moment they can snatch. They do it riding to work or at home. They take fifteen minutes from the time usually spent in profitless reading or amusement. The results really are phenomenal.

Sherwin Cody has placed an excellent command of the English language within the grasp of everyone. Those who take advantage of his method gain something so priceless that it cannot be measured in terms of money. They gain a mark of breeding that cannot be erased as long as they live. They gain a facility in speech that marks them as educated people in whatever society they find themselves. They gain the self-confidence and self-respect which this ability inspires. As for material reward, certainly the importance of good English in the race for success cannot be over-estimated. Surely, no one can advance far without it.

FREE — Book on English

It is impossible in this brief review, to give more than a suggestion of the range of subjects covered by Mr. Cody's new method and of what his practice exercises consist. But those who are interested can find a detailed description in a fascinating little book called "How You Can Master Good English in 15 Minutes a Day." This is published by the Sherwin Cody School of English in Rochester. It can be had by anyone, free upon request. There is no obligation involved in writing for it. The book is more than a prospectus. Unquestionably, it tells one of the most interesting stories about education in English ever written.

If you are interested in learning more in detail of what Sherwin Cody can do for you, send for the book "How You Can Master Good English in 15 Minutes a Day."

Merely mail the coupon, a letter or postal card for it now. No agent will call. SHERWIN CODY SCHOOL OF ENGLISH, 8811 B. & O. Building, Rochester 4, N. Y.

QUESTIONS I'VE BEEN ASKED FREQUENTLY -- and my answers.

Q. Can a letter that presents the proposition clearly and sincerely, but does not follow the classic sales formula (Attention, Interest, Conviction, and Action), ever be a successful letter?

No. If a letter doesn't attract attention, how can it generate interest? And if it isn't interesting, how can it create desire? And if no desire to own is created, what good would convincing do? And if all these criteria are not created first, how can it compel to action? A new formula for selling may come along in time, but I doubt it will ever equal the old one of attention, interest, conviction, action.

Q. Does the date on your letter have a strong and compelling value?

Unless your letter capitalizes on a specific date, making an offer good for 10 days from date, I would never date a letter beyond the month or the year. With the mails what they are, a dated letter may be dated indeed by the time it gets to its destination. It's what you say that really counts, not the minute or day you said it.

Q. When, in writing a long letter, you explain the special offer forcefully and in great detail at the close, should you also mention it near the opening?

Human nature is the same whatever sales method is used.

Generally speaking I would bring the offer in near the beginning of the letter. If you have ever listened to a typical pitchman you will remember that he always promised enough at the beginning of his pitch to hold his audience. He may have held dollar bills aloft in his fingers, or promised to give something away free, but he always had a gimmick that riveted you to the spot until he told you his whole selling story. Human nature is the same whatever sales method is used.

Q. When writing letters to businessmen, should the letter take on a more formal and serious tone?

A "half price sale" is just as appealing to doctors and lawyers as it is to foundry and mill workers.

The most important thing to remember is that businessmen, doctors, lawyers, book-lovers, prospects of any kind, are first of all people. "90 days free trial" is just as effective in selling computers and software as it is in selling shaving cream and tooth paste. A "half price sale" is just as appealing to doctors and lawyers as it is to foundry and mill workers. It won't take the average businessman more than two seconds to find out what you're up to -- whether you write your letter by hand, individually type it, or process it. He wants to know WHO, WHAT, WHERE AND FOR HOW MUCH! No matter how you slice it and serve it up he wants to know whether it's ham or cheese. My feeling is, use any device that will attract him and hold his attention. However, I would never sacrifice selling force for dignity.

Q. The ad writer tends to get tired of writing the same phrase in the same way. "ACT TODAY" is written so often it seems worked to death and may therefore lose maximum effectiveness. Should the writer try to be more original?

It is dangerous to insult the intelligence of your readers.

By all means use new phrases to express old thoughts. But don't reach into the realm of the incredible to make your copy different. It is dangerous to insult the intelligence of your readers -- and is wholly unnecessary. If you can't say anything else to get action, simply remind the reader of the number of things he intended to do in the past but "forgot". Stick pretty close to the things the reader knows -- and your hurry up won't sound fishy.

Q. How important is the product to the sales story?

Your product is your best copy. If you have a good product that will produce results for the buyer, your copy will almost write itself. Build your sales appeal around those results and then target the right market -- qualified prospects.

Q. How important is your offer?

Your offer can make a hero or a bum out of the finest, slickest string of words you ever turned out. We'll talk more about this in later pages.

UNDERSTANDING THE BASICS OF ADVERTISING

For in the final analysis advertising is selling.

The basics of good copy is to think in terms of words that sell, for in the final analysis advertising is selling.

1. Concentrate on the consumer. In the end you must sell him no matter what method you use. And to do that, you must know how he thinks.

2. Know your product -- its material, its manufacture, its use. Those are the **features.**

3. Find the symptom or symptoms that your product is qualified to "cure". The cure is the **benefit.** It may be a mental, physical or financial benefit (that cures a symptom), but your product must have an excuse for its existence.

4. Never start to write a sales letter or ad until you have first built up an avalanche of enthusiasm for the task at hand. Your writing must be exciting!

It should inform, enlighten, instruct or promise a reward.

5. Advertising is essentially news. It should inform, enlighten, instruct or promise a reward. The news may take many forms. It may be price. It may be a new slant on quality or both. It may be a new cure for an old malady. It may be a new way to use an old product. It may be startling language applied to a prosaic product. But advertising is always more potent if you can also include interesting news.

C - O - P - Y

C - is for CONCEPT. A term used widely in the advertising and marketing industry. It translates into "original idea" or scheme. The Disneyland CONCEPT was built around a carnival atmosphere using Disney movie scenes and characters depicting living entities.

O - is for OFFER. The very most important aspect of any sales letter concerns the description of what the company proposes to trade for the prospect's money. Usually the main product or service plus several enticing gifts or bonuses. The OFFER can also include easy payment plans; guarantee of satisfaction or money back; holding customer's check for a certain time period to ensure satisfaction; or any other transactional appeals. The better your OFFER, the more sales you'll make.

P - is for PRICE of PRODUCT (or service) being offered. The most attractive PRODUCT in the world will not sell in sufficient quantity if the PRICE does not equal the customer's **perceived** value. Let your copy give a believable reason for offering a price discount "at this time". Let the market tell you your best asking price. Test several different prices in a direct mail split run TEST.

Y - is for "YOU" and "YOUR". The two words that attract the prospect's eye. Next in importance, only to using his or her own name in the body copy.

CHAPTER THREE

TESTING

After 75 years of pushing an advertising pencil, of scheming sales schemes, of juggling words and thoughts -- after all these years of testing, mailing and analyzing -- I have come to the conclusion that mail order people generally are addicted to the insidious habit of over testing and "under thinking".

He believes the easiest and surest way out of any selling problem is to test.

So serious is this disease that in its most pernicious form the unsuspecting victim loses his normal, natural ability to judge fairly, to make sound decisions, to act wisely. His muscles of wisdom become atrophied and his power of discrimination calcifies. He believes the easiest and surest way out of any selling problem is to test. Why **think** when it is so easy to get the correct answers by mailing a couple of thousand, or by running an ad or two?

And the element of elapsed time is only one of the dangers.

But, is testing the key to personal success or may it, like fire, be a good thing only if there isn't too much of it? The truth is, if every test could be safely projected much of the fallacy of testing would be eliminated. We know how much difference there can be between a test and a mailing -- or between the result of a single ad and a full campaign! Too many things happen in these fast-moving times to destroy the projection of a test. Within the span of a season, a month, or even a week, marked economic, competitive or psychological changes can take place and when they do ..... blooie go your expectations. And the element of elapsed time is only one of the dangers.

Testing is important, but even more important, is the necessity for exercising good judgment after making the tests. After so many years of recorded experience, I have learned testing does not always tell the whole truth. We will never completely formularize advertising as long as there are changes in the weather, in world conditions, in domestic affairs, and even in local conditions from month to month and from week to week. We will never be able to trust the results of a test with absolute assurance and certainty.

This is not an argument against testing, but against faulty interpretations of tests. I object to tests which determine the best day of the week on which to mail; tests which are intended to prove whether a price of $5.98 is better than $5.99. Tests of 500 or even 1000 to determine whether a proposition or a list is worth rolling out on a scale of 10 thousand or 10 million! Tests that tell you nothing or actually mislead you are worse than none. Divide any mailing list into units of 1000, and after the results are in, check the percentages of orders against each of those units. You'll often be startled by the difference between your "best" thousand names and your "worst".

Why do ninety-five percent of the people you reach turn you down?

If your mailings bring in two, three or even five percent of orders, there must be something wrong. Why do ninety-five percent of the people you reach turn you down? Even though the percentage you get is highly profitable, is that any reason to shudder at the possibility of doubling it? The natural tendency is to analyze why the 5% <u>did</u> order, which might uncover a way to reach more of the same kind of people.

After all, those who buy are 100% sold. All we need is more like them!

It's useless to ask people why they didn't buy. **They simply don't know!** In several mail questionnaires, and many personal polls, we found that the conscious answers people gave for not buying were pure bunk. But people do have a definite reason for buying -- and you'll get the right answer by asking them.

Confine your tests to important changes, not trivial ones. You will never get the exact same answers over again.

The cure for indiscriminate testing is judgment. You must discard ruthlessly and boldly; without regret or reservation, any idea you are not confident has a chance to pay. Confine your tests to important changes, not trivial ones. As long as you are doing direct mail you will never get the exact same answers over again. Exercise your muscles of thinking instead of leaning entirely on "physical" crutches. It's good for you to stand or fall on your best judgment. It will give you confidence when you are proved right, and it will teach you invaluable lessons when you are proved wrong. You can always hang onto what you're doing until a big change comes along. Go for the big deal or you may become so confused by small differences in results that you will lose your perspective and your ability to exercise your God-given asset of judgment. Life is too short to spend dotting the "i's" and crossing the "t's". Test important offers, new products, broader distribution of your mailings, more restricted coverage, or changes in prices. But forget about minor details -- you'll save yourself a lot of time and agony trying to apply the results of such tests. Do more of your business by ear, by instinct, by logic and less by cold hard figures.

Research in advance can help determine these factors.

The right selection and proper use of lists is vital to the success of any mail order proposition, so make sure your mailings are appropriate to your product, to your audience and to conditions. Research in advance can help determine these factors.

A more careful screening of lists before you test may be in order. With postage rates up, and everything else too, less waste of time, money and material may be the road to survival. You might begin this wave of screening right at home -- on your own list. Keep it cleaner than you ever kept it before. It may pay you to check outside lists against your own -- even against each other. (One big mailer I know of hires out-of-town college students to cross off the slum district streets in their own home cities before they mail.)

We must thank the advertising agency of Crall, Mack & Macfadden for discovering, in the early 1880's, that cute little device known as the key-numbering system, which enables us to determine the relative effectiveness of different headlines, offers, media and other important elements in our campaign. However, even after testing, testing, and more testing, we must remember that computers compute but even they can't **think**. Electronic equipment adds, subtracts, multiplies, divides, sorts, classifies and tabulates with speed of light but your own brain must resolve matters that depend on judgment.

The end of testing is only the beginning of your real problem.

The reason for many failures is not a lack of ideas, but a lack of discrimination in their use. You will never rise to the heights you dream about until your judgment becomes the master instead of the slave of any testing you do ... for, in the final analysis the end of testing is only the beginning of your real problem.

So stop gambling so much on a "sure thing" in mail order.

You must follow your successful tests with successful management programs, keeping an open mind as to when to "quit". So stop gambling so much even on a "sure thing" in mail order. Use your head instead of trusting in luck. Temper your tests with good judgment!

QUESTIONS AND ANSWERS

Q. Is there any special formula for quantities of names to be tested?

This depends on the size of each list and a judgment as to where to reach a point of stability in results. The importance of an accurate result would also determine the quantity to be tested. Usually a test of 2,000 is sufficient where 2% results will tell the story. If only 1% is required, probably a minimum test of 5,000 should be considered. The danger is more on the side of making an inadequate test than on the side of making elaborate tests. So much effort and money goes into the preparatory cost of a mailing, it seems criminal to use small tests which may conflict or be too small to bring in a stable percentage of results.

The mailing list, itself, is of utmost importance. Make every list owner tell you more precisely what you are getting!

Q. How many names are considered adequate for a reliable test?

This can usually be worked backwards. Figure on getting a minimum of 100 orders. That means, if 1% is needed because of the margin of profit, 10,000 can be tested. If 2% is needed, test 5,000 names. If the deal is such that 5% is needed to bring in 100 orders, test 2,000. There's too much risk in judging results by 10, 15, 25 or perhaps even 50 orders. A few orders more or less may make a tremendous difference in your percentages. Make your tests worthwhile.

Q. In testing a new product, is it a good idea to test first using a space advertisement or to prepare a mailing piece and test using logical lists?

The best test, of course, is to try both simultaneously.

Much depends upon the product and the publicity it is advisable to give to launching it. I think a space test is faster and more reliable because many more people can be reached for the same amount of money. However, the best test, of course, is to try both simultaneously. I would not rely on either unless the test was clearly successful. Too many mailings fall down while ads pay. I certainly would try both if the mathematics of the deal made success feasible.

Successful advertising has no secret springs, no trap doors, no hidden panels. It's simply a selling problem; and if properly fathomed and engineered, a simple selling problem.

-- Maxwell B. Sackheim

CHAPTER FOUR

THE SEVEN DEADLY MAIL ORDER MISTAKES

MISTAKE #1

Offer The Wrong Merchandise -- Whether Goods Or Services:

The first, and most important consideration is what you are trying to sell. Is it light in weight in proportion to its price? Except for other disadvantages, the ideal product for mail order selling would be a diamond. It is ideally light and ideally expensive. The worst product is probably an anvil for the reverse reasons. Your mail order product must not be handicapped by excessive transportation charges in proportion to its total cost.

CHECKLIST -- Ask Yourself:

Is it something new -- or something old with a new twist?

Is it a bargain, not necessarily price-wise but in what it does to or for the customer? In simpler words, does the advertising practically write itself because the product sells itself?

Is the price and the unit of profit high enough so that you don't have to get repeat business, or is the product one that repeats often enough so the original selling cost is not the determining factor?

Is the product simple, or is it likely to need repairs which may be difficult to obtain and which may scare prospective buyers away? Is it easily breakable in the mail? Are colors and sizes involved which will cause resistance and returns? Is there an inventory or warehouse problem?

Is there any evidence that the product is wanted by a large enough audience to make mail order feasible?

Is your purpose other than orders? If so, what are you trying to accomplish and what is par for your course? By what standards are you going to measure results?

If you are wrong in your selection of merchandise, you are licked before you start.

MISTAKE #2

Offer Merchandise At The Wrong Price:

The lowest price never gets all the business!

By wrong price I don't mean a price that isn't competitive. The lowest price never gets all the business! Many small general stores are open from 7 a.m. to 11 p.m. daily and Sunday. Their prices are a few cents higher, yet they do a nice business because they render a service which on many occasions is more important than price.

What is important is your unit price and your margin of profit. If your price is too high for normal, natural direct mail sale, you must have compensating factors such as shipments on approval, time payments, a wide-open guarantee backed by unquestioned sponsorship, or a name like Sears, Wards, Tiffany, or Neiman-Marcus. You might even be better off trying to make the sale in two jumps, obtaining inquiries first and then following up with the big expensive pitch, or even with a live salesman, if possible.

Beware of the small unit, short margin mail order item.

The most dangerous price mistake is to have too low a unit of margin. Even if your tests show satisfactory results, have you allowed for a sufficient safety factor to warrant a large mailing? It's fine if cash is not important; if you have a substantial bank account and can wait for repeat business. But if your budget is limited, if you have no other source of revenue or your sales are likely to be far apart, beware of the small unit, short margin mail order item. Of course, you can test anything but temper your testing with good judgment. You don't want to run out of cash before you find the right answer.

MISTAKE #3

The Wrong Offer:

This is one of the most deadly. I've mentioned wrong price, but a wrong offer can wreck the right price. For example, an open-account offer on a low priced item might bring in a fantastic number of orders but after you deduct bad debts, cost of collections and bookkeeping expense, you might be better off with a much smaller cash business. On the other hand, a high priced item might demand an open account offer, or time payments, or some other compensating inducement or incentive to buy by mail.

Offers include many factors other than price. I came across an old mail order ad written for a paint manufacturer. The ad offered enough paint for a house -- one, two or three coats. All you had to do was send the dimensions of your home and a price would be quoted, not by the gallon but for enough paint to do the whole job! The paint manufacturer guaranteed, at the price quoted, you would have some paint left over when the job was finished.

The unusual thing about this offer was that no price was mentioned!

An old-time cosmetic manufacturer offered to send a jar of face cream on approval -- pay in 10 days if satisfied. The unusual thing about this offer was that no price was mentioned! With the package you got a bill and that was the first knowledge you had of the price. The plan must have worked for he kept it up for many years.

I mentioned these incidents to show that new and ingenious offers can be developed. A good offer, I might even say, can be priceless!

MISTAKE #4

Wrong Timing:

It's a mistake to mail too early, but it's a calamity to mail too late. How far in advance of using-time should you mail? If your product is used in April, test in January. If purchased or used at Christmas, or as a Christmas gift, test your product as early as September. As soon as your test results justify the roll-out, shoot the works with the big campaign!

If you mail early, perhaps you can squeeze in a profitable follow-up mailing after your original mailing has gone out. One of our friends makes three Christmas gift mailings -- one in September which pays, one in October which also pays, and the last one about November 10th which has paid in the past.

Regardless of use-time, some months are poor-reading months. April, May and June are notably bad even for red-hot summer items simply because these are poor reading months. December is bad except for priority-mail gift orders.

A good share of new business comes from the most recent buyers!

Wrong timing also applies to customer mailings. How soon after receiving an order should you solicit another order? My answer is -- **often.** Send catalogs every year to all your customers and your business will be multiplied. A good share of new business comes from the most recent buyers!

MISTAKE #5

The Use Of Wrong Lists:

The best lists are, of course, your own live customer names and your own inquiries. Next are lists of other people's customers who have bought related merchandise (preferably by mail) and finally, any kind of **mail order buyer.** You can rent the use of many of these lists or trade the use of your list for theirs. (Consult a list broker for detailed information about logical lists for your use.)

Good lists are the life-blood of the mail order business. The wrong list can sound the death knell of an otherwise good venture. Choose your lists with care, and test only to the extent that you can afford to lose.

MISTAKE #6

The Wrong Format:

Where do we begin and where do we end? Shall we use a government postcard? Or shall we go all out with a letter, a four-color brochure, a catalog, a beautiful order form, a big priority mail outgoing envelope, a smaller Business Reply return envelope? In the idiom of Abraham Lincoln, a mailing, like a man's legs, should be "long enough to reach the ground". In other words, it should be adequate -- not so expensive as to make the required number of responses beyond the pale of reason and experience, and not so cheap and unattractive as to get the waste basket treatment at first glance. A moderately priced item laced with a comfortable profit margin might benefit from two or more colors on a slick paper like a 60# coated stock. But if the margin of profit is very small, the sender might do better with plain old 20# bond, either white or one of the standard colors like buff, golden rod, ivory, pale pink or pale blue.

The very simplicity of his mailing is news and smacks of a bargain!

I received a mailing from a company that sells nylon stockings by mail. Now, any woman, anywhere can buy any size, any color of nylons (panty-hose) at a price she wants to pay. Nylons are always on sale everywhere -- in drug, department and stationery stores, even through vending machines. Yet this fellow sells them by mail under the very noses of local merchants. How does he do it? Does he have a very fancy mailing? Does he offer to ship on open account? Are his prices amazingly low? No! His mailing is one of the most inexpensive it is possible to produce -- just a circular cheaply printed. All he does is price his nylons by the dozen and make every recipient feel like an "agent" not a customer. He makes his presentation fit the psychology of his prospects. The very simplicity of his mailing is news and smacks of a bargain! His unit is high enough to make his percentage requirement possible and he does a fine repeat business.

MISTAKE #7

Bad Management:

"Mail order" is not a business in itself. It is a way of doing business.

If you have every other qualification for success, your house of cards is still bound to collapse if your business is poorly managed. In mail order marketing, practically every known business requirement must be observed. We must buy. We must sell. We must finance. We must advertise. We must fulfill. We must collect. We must control inventory. We usually must warehouse. Sometimes we must even invent and manufacture. And yet you must understand that "mail order" is not a business in itself. It is a **way of doing business.**

Hire mail order as you would a master salesman.

The surest and safest way to get into "mail order" is as the by-product of a successful, on-going business which now sells in other ways. If you have a business that is making money, put mail order on your payroll at so much a week or month or a year, just as you would a new salesman who has made a reputation in some other line or with some other company. You would give him a chance to make good even if you lost money on him for a while. You would hire him to tell your sales story convincingly, without leaving any important selling points out, and yet not going into so much superfluous detail that he loses the prospect's interest ... and finally, to hand the pen to the prospect and indicate where he should sign to place the order. The necessity of writing the check is automatically understood beyond that point. Hire mail order as you would a master salesman. And if you are not adept at it now, study the fine points by reading books such as this one.

There are many more than Seven Deadly Mail Order Mistakes, but there are also many more than Seven Great Mail Order Rewards.

CHAPTER FIVE

USING IMAGINATION CREATIVELY

And I'm sure the same process goes on in the minds of today's most brilliant advertising people.

Every advertising man I ever knew or heard of, including John E. Kennedy, Claude Hopkins, Lynn Sumner, Wilbur Ruthrauff, David Ogilvy, John Caples, Leo Burnett and others in advertising's Hall of Fame, adapted, applied, altered, combined and otherwise utilized two or more old ideas to produce new ones. And I'm sure the same process goes on in the minds of today's most brilliant advertising people. I'd like to wrap this process up in one word -- IMAGINATION.

What is this process? Must we emulate Rodin's statue of "The Thinker"? Is it the child of wrinkled brows, dreams, solitude, hypnotism? Not at all. It's the gathering and recycling of facts, elements, experiences, history -- and arranging them in patterns to fit more modern human wants. All you need is a mind that is open, eyes that see, ears that hear, a memory that clicks, curiosity enough to make your brain a catalyst and courage enough to risk ridicule.

A fertile field for IMAGINATION is the challenge of getting the most out of current customers, and customers not so current. One way used by most mail order people is to get them to send in names of friends. Another is to offer them a reward for getting new customers. One large mail order advertiser does as much as 30% of his total business through a customer-get-a-customer plan.

Another challenge to the imagination is the use of riders -- those little squares at the bottom of your coupon or order form to offer an innocent little change in the customer's order -- like a small bonus for cash in advance instead of an open account, or to buy a higher priced item than the one featured, or to subscribe for multiple years instead of only one.

It can actually make a mailing profitable instead of unprofitable.

At least 10% and as high as 25% of your orders can be for the "rider" you offer. It can actually make a mailing profitable instead of unprofitable. You might even try several riders. It is a fallacy to think that the more offers you make the more confused the prospect will be. Long ago smart publishers found that many people bought books which were merely listed on an order form even though the entire mailing was about some other book. The title alone sold them without any other salesmanship, and so additional sales were made **because of a rider**.

As a public service, we prepared a fund raising campaign for a local YMCA. Instead of soliciting memberships in the usual way, we mailed signed trial membership cards to every prospect on our list. They didn't join us, we joined them! All they had to do to validate their membership was place an "X" in the little box which designated the type of member they wanted to become on a trial basis and send in the remittance according to the schedule. This may be an adaptation of unordered merchandise mailings, but we did qualify it by asking the prospect to please destroy the membership card if it wasn't wanted -- we didn't ask for its return! Results were very good.

But it took IMAGINATION to apply them to mail order.

You have undoubtedly received mailings containing stamps or perforated punch-out tokens, good for this or that. They have been used for many, many years by various non-profit organizations in fund raising mailings -- but it took IMAGINATION to apply them to mail order sales efforts.

That famous Reader's Digest mailing in which two pennies were enclosed.

It also took imagination to come up with that famous Reader's Digest mailing in which two pennies were enclosed (your change in advance from $3 because the price was only $2.98).

Somewhat the same thought seems to be present when a prospect is asked to answer yes or no to a presentation. There is, of course, no obligation to do either but given a choice one is more apt

"Always make it easier to say 'yes' than to say 'no'."

to do something than nothing -- and that extra moment of consideration apparently shifts more to "yes" answers than to "no" answers! In the parlance of some of my master salesmen friends: "Always make it easier to say 'yes' than to say 'no'." In example, that's why we always furnish a postage pre-paid Business Reply Envelope, an 800 phone number, and a charge card acceptance policy. All of these make it easier to say yes to a direct response sales offer.

In the early days, before these tools were invented, a buyer who decided to order from a mail order firm would have to 1). Clip the coupon out of the magazine. 2). Fill in their name, address, city, state and item's order # or name. 3). Find an envelope. 4). Address it. 5). Make out the check. 6). Stuff and seal the envelope. 7). Walk to the mail box and drop sealed order in. And finally, wait for weeks for the slow mail delivery.

Today, with FAX and charge card orders by telephone, the order can be placed in a matter of seconds simply by punching in a toll-free phone number. And the fulfillment will be done usually on the same working day. That's what I call making it "easier to say yes than to say no".

You can always find a new angle to an old business or a new business with an old angle.

I have no idea when the sweepstakes or prize contest vogue will wear out, if ever, but most retailers have not found it necessary to resort to these gimmicks. Indeed one of our most successful chain store operators gave up on the use of yellow or green stamps and business increased tremendously -- not because he discontinued giving stamps but perhaps because he used other incentives. The busiest gas station in one area offered a choice of 1 cent per gallon discount or stamps. Most of the patrons preferred the cash discount, so keep thinking about new membership services, new combination offers, yes even a new kind of premium. Just don't stay put in the face of pressure being brought to bear on you. You can always find a new angle to an old business or a new business with an old angle. One modern chain of gas stations, AM-PM, offers a large plastic coffee mug that will not spill if tipped over in the car -- at a discounted price when you fill up your tank.

Another example:

Instead of asking for the dollar in advance, she said "send no money".

Many years ago a Kansas City mail order expert was selling a vitamin tonic for poultry intended to induce or enable hens to lay more eggs. It was sold exclusively by mail at $1 a package, cash in advance. Attracted by the tremendous volume of advertising he was doing, competitors soon appeared. Among them was a lady who couldn't beat his claims but did beat his sales plan by borrowing an idea from another mail order company. Instead of asking for the dollar in advance, she said "send no money - pay the postman when the package arrives". The same plan was being used successfully by an old timer who owned a mail order dress company in Chicago -- who copied the idea from a fellow named Sears who used it as far back as 1898. Sears sold watches by mail and shipped by express -- all charges collect!

In 1914 Harry Scherman and I published a series of pocket-size classics which sold for 10 cents each. After months of experimenting we decided to try selling them in sets by mail. We tested ads in the old *Pathfinder* magazine and what do you think the best headline was?

"SEND NO MONEY!"

In about 3 years we sold over 40,000,000 of those books!

One of our more clever offers --

In our direct mail effort we borrowed an idea from an auctioneer. We enclosed a small sample of the cover material used on our little books, and a short letter which started something like this, "how much would you guess 30 books bound in the material enclosed should sell for to be a sensational bargain?" The letter listed the 30 titles, described the cover material, gave some other details, asked the reader to write his guess down and then to break the seal to see what the actual price was.

THE GREATEST BARGAIN OF YOUR LIFE

$2.98

FOR ALL

THIRTY WORLD'S GREATEST

MASTERPIECES

We believed the American public would appreciate an opportunity to purchase THIRTY of the greatest books ever written, for only $2.98. But we were amazed at the enthusiastic response. Letters pour in every day praising the books, praising the offer, ordering additional sets. Think of it. Thirty wonderful Books for only $2.98.

Flexible Redcroft Binding

A year's reading of the most wonderful books ever written! $2.98 for ALL THIRTY—not for ONE —NOT A FIRST PAYMENT. Each book complete—NOT EXTRACTS. Each volume printed in clear, readable type, on excellent book paper, and bound in wonderful flexible Redcroft —looks and wears better than leather. Over FOUR MILLION VOLUMES HAVE BEEN SOLD WITHOUT ADVERTISING.

SEND NO MONEY

Just mail coupon or letter. These are the wonderful Little Leather Library books which are so convenient in size. You can carry one in your pocket wherever you go. World's greatest authors, including Kipling, De Maupassant, Stevenson, Oscar Wilde, Edgar Allan Poe, Shakespeare, Lincoln, Irving, Conan Doyle, Emerson, Thoreau, Burns, Henry Drummond, Omar Khayyam, Browning and others. All 30 vols. for only $2.98.

Mail coupon and we will send the entire 30 volumes at once. Simply pay postman $2.98 plus postage, and examine the books for 30 days. The publisher of this magazine guarantees REFUND if you are not more than pleased. At this price of $2.98 they will be cleaned out quickly. Mail coupon or copy it in a letter at once.

LITTLE
LEATHER
LIBRARY
CORP'N
Dept. 384
354 – 4th Ave.
New York City,
N. Y.

Little Leather Library Corp'n
Dept. 384
354 - 4th Ave.
New York City,
N. Y.

Please send me the 30 volumes of world's greatest masterpieces, bound in flexible Redcroft. I will pay the postman $2.98 plus postage but if I am not satisfied I will mail the books back at your expense within 30 days and you are to refund my money at once, It is distinctly understood that there are no further payments.

Name..............................

Address..............................

.... (Outside U. S. Price $3.98 cash with order.) ....

WASHINGTON'S SPEECHES AND LETTERS

THE TEMPEST

BALLAD OF READING GAOL

POEMS – BROWNING

SHERLOCK HOLMES

MAN WITHOUT A COUNTRY

GREATEST THING IN THE WORLD

FIFTY BEST POEMS OF ENGLAND

MIDSUMMER NIGHT'S DREAM

FRIENDSHIP AND OTHER ESSAYS-THOREAU

THE ANCIENT MARINER

LINCOLN'S SPEECHES AND ADDRESSES

THE HAPPY PRINCE

BARRACK ROOM BALLADS

POEMS – BURNS

FIFTY BEST POEMS OF AMERICA

SALOME - WILDE

WILL O'THE MILL - STEVENSON

THE GOLD BUG

ENOCH ARDEN

BAB BALLADS

LAYS OF ANCIENT ROME

THE RUBAIYAT OF OMAR KHAYYAM

EMERSON'S ESSAYS

DREAMS

DR JEKYLL AND MR HYDE

COURTSHIP OF MILES STANDISH

A CHILD'S GARDEN OF VERSES

THE COMING OF ARTHUR

SHORT STORIES – DE MAUPASSANT

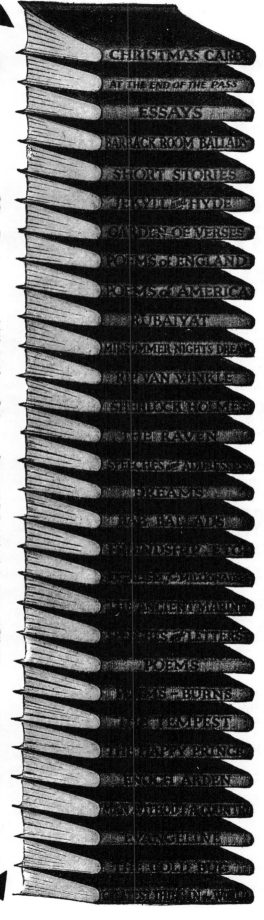

You can imagine the impact of the $2.98 price if the reader bid $5, $7.50, $10 or even $50 which a few did. We didn't do the selling -- the prospect sold himself, just as the patrons of auctions do!

Birth of the "OF-THE MONTH CLUB"

Eventually the sale of our little books slowed down, and we tested what we called an easy way to obtain a literary education for only $4.98 by offering to mail a classic a week for a year on subscription. We called the enterprise **"Book-of the-Week Club"** -- but we found that we couldn't afford to wait a year to complete a $4.98 sale.

We then switched to offering sets of phonograph records by mail, including a set of sacred songs, another of grand opera selections, still another of old time American folk songs and finally a set of popular hits headed by the popular hit song of that time "Yes, We Have No Bananas". When our phonograph record sales reached a million dollars a year and bananas were plentiful again, we sold the business to the record manufacturer and our thoughts returned to selling books.

Now we had four elements to combine out of our experience.

Now we had four elements to combine out of our experience: Send no money; the subscription method of obtaining automatic resales; the tremendous sale of new popular records as compared with that of classics, and the importance of establishing a worthwhile value. Out of this conglomeration was born **"Book-of-the-Month Club"**. But even this was not a new idea! Actually Benjamin Franklin organized the first subscription library in the colonies in 1731. And before Book-of-the-Month Club began distribution of its first selection, Ben Huebsch (a prominent publisher of that day) wrote, "Of all the recent developments in book production, none is quite so significant as the German book clubs..." which as far back as 1919 offered reprints and cheap editions of the classics at a price almost anyone could afford. And a fellow by the name of Samuel Craig claimed to have formulated and officially incorporated the plan of the *Literary Guild* in April 1922 -- although this organization did not begin operations until January 1927.

Two Book-of-the-Month Club ads on the following pages.

Placed in your hand *so* that you can't miss it

~ *the outstanding book each month!*

Henry Seidel Canby

THE average person *fails to read* most of the outstanding books published. He misses them because he is either *too busy* or *too neglectful* to go out and buy them. How often has this happened to you? "I certainly want to read *that* book!" you say to yourself, when you see a review or hear a book praised highly. But, in most cases, you never "get around to it."

The Book-of-the-Month Club takes cognizance of this procrastination that forever causes you to miss the best books; *each month, if you decide you want it, you receive an outstanding new book published that month—just as you receive a magazine—by mail!*

Christopher Morley

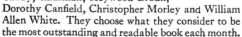

How is this "outstanding" book chosen and how do you decide whether or not you want it? Each month, the new books, *of all publishers,* are presented to our Selecting Committee which consists of Henry Seidel Canby, chairman; Heywood Broun, Dorothy Canfield, Christopher Morley and William Allen White. They choose what they consider to be the most outstanding and readable book each month.

Dorothy Canfield

Heywood Broun

You will concede that a book selected by such a group is *likely* to be one that you would not care to miss reading. But you may disagree with their choice in any one month. For that reason, before the book comes to you (remember it has not yet been published) you receive a clear and illuminating report upon

it. If you want it, you let it come to you. If not, you specify that some other book be sent instead, making your choice from a list of other new and important books, which are also reported upon fully. Even if you let the book come to you, and find yourself disappointed, you may exchange it for any other book you prefer.

Thus, not only are you absolutely safeguarded against missing the books you want to read; you also keep completely informed about all the worth-while new books; and you exercise a more discriminating choice among the new books than you do now.

The cost of this unique service is—nothing. You pay only for the books you take, and for them you pay the same price as if you got them from the publisher himself, by mail.

If you are interested in this service, and wish to know more about it, send for our prospectus. Your request will involve you in no obligation to subscribe.

Wm. Allen White

BOOK-OF-THE-MONTH CLUB, INC.   4-J
218 West 40th Street, New York

Please send me, without cost, your Prospectus outlining the details of the Book-of-the-Month Plan. This request involves me in no obligation to subscribe to your service.

Name _____

Address _____

City _____ State _____

You get only the books you want and pay only for those you keep

—when you belong to the Book-of-the-Month Club. That is why over 90,000 discriminating readers belong to this organization

WE feel it is only fair to ourselves to advise book readers about the distinction between the Book-of-the-Month Club and other organizations that have arisen since it started. The chief function of the Club is—not to select books for you that you must accept and pay for, whether you like them or not; *but to prevent you from missing the particular new books that you decide you want to read.*

Be honest with yourself: how frequently do you fail to get and read an important worth-while book which everybody else is reading and discussing?

Our system, once for all, will not only effectually prevent this for you, but you will become one of the first readers of the important new books. You do not receive twelve specific books a year, which you are obliged to keep and pay for; you receive carefully written, authoritative reports, *in advance of publication*, upon from 150 to 200 books a year—winnowed out, from the thousands published, by a group of judges upon whom you can rely; and the books among these that you decide you must read, *you get without fail*—under our system. You can't overlook or forget about them, as you now do so frequently.

This sensible service—there is no other like it—is undoubtedly the reason why there are more book-readers who belong to the Book-of-the-Month Club—over 90,000 now, and the number grows monthly—than to all the many other book clubs in this country combined.

It costs you nothing to join. There are no fees, no dues, no charges of any kind. You pay only for the books you take. Find out how our system operates, and about its many conveniences that cannot be described here for lack of space. Your request for information involves you in no obligation.

Henry Seidel Canby
Chairman

Heywood
Broun

Dorothy
Canfield

Christopher
Morley

William Allen
White

THE SELECTING COMMITTEE OF THE BOOK-OF-THE-MONTH CLUB

Somehow the public manages to put most uninspired enterprises out of business.

I have no idea how many "of-the-month" clubs have started since Book-of-the-Month Club was launched, but there must have been several hundred such ventures. Most, if not all, are gone and forgotten. This is not to say there isn't room for other successful "of-the-month" ideas, but it should emphasize the importance of the factors necessary for success in any enterprise. The graveyard of hopes for success is filled with products and companies which were backed by costly advertising and adequate financing but not by the necessary imagination, quality, value, service and proper business management. Somehow the public manages to put most uninspired enterprises out of business.

IMAGINATION created giant post card mailings with a business reply card attached. Imagination created multiple mailings. Imagination will create the sale of more multiple units through club plans, wholesale efforts, and discount pricing. Imagination will lead to more inquiry mailings, sampling, time limit offers, customer-get-customer mailings and a whole raft of new selling ideas which may be the result of putting two or more old selling ideas together.

Every advertising man is familiar with the phrase "my business is different".

Every advertising man is familiar with the phrase "my business is different". Nearly every time I have tried to convince an advertiser that a plan which has worked successfully in another business might work successfully in his, he has at least thought, if he did not say it, that his business is different. But old and used ideas can be adapted to **any business.**

It has been said that necessity is the mother of invention. Far be it from me to disturb this thought, but I cannot reconcile it with the invention of many products which are not as necessary as the wheel, or electricity, or the internal combustion engine. In every area of our lives countless products of the imagination became necessities **after** they were produced. Advertising played its part in accomplishing this, by raising our standard of living.

Use your IMAGINATION -- and imagine what it can do for you!

CHAPTER SIX

THE NEGATIVE OPTION PLAN

The main enemies of advertising.

The enemies of advertising are INDIFFERENCE, APATHY and INERTIA. Indifference is normal. Our attitude toward nearly everything we see, read, hear and experience is "So what?". Indifference is the number one hurdle advertisers must overcome.

One stand-up comic uses the line "Who cares about apathy?". That's an ironic look at contemporary life in America.

You begin to appreciate what a hurdle indifference is when you realize how terrific the competition is for your prospect's time and attention.

Inertia is the other built-in obstacle we must fight. Inertia is the law of physics which declares that a body in motion or at rest resists change. People hate to bother changing their minds, their habits, their routines, or their opinions. It takes tons of persuasion to make people do even the things they want to do! That's why we have one-day sales and other **limited-time** offers, and do all sorts of things to get people to overcome that deadly enemy of action - inertia!

My dictionary gives this description of INERTIA --

1. **[Physics.] The tendency of a body to resist acceleration; the tendency of a body at rest to remain at rest or of a body in motion to stay in motion in a straight line unless acted on by an outside force.**

2. **Resistance or disinclination to motion, action, or change: the inertia of an entrenched bureaucracy.**

The principle of "inertia" in selling (or now the so-called "negative option plan") goes back to the time when Richard W. Sears sold watches by mail in 1898. In those days, the watches were shipped by express with the added privilege of examination before paying. No money was requested in advance.

This theory was used in formulating the sales plan for our Book-of-the-Month Club.

This theory was used in formulating the sales plan for our Book-of-the-Month Club. In its infancy there were so many cancellations and returns (by the carload) it became necessary to change the plan radically. That was when I decided we should notify subscribers in advance of the book selected, giving a comprehensive description and allowing a respectable period in which to refuse the selection or substitute for another if they did not want to receive the book selected by the Editorial Board.

The "negative option plan" was started with one thought in mind.

The "negative option plan" was started with one thought in mind; that of removing resistance on the part of the prospect to order merchandise which he wanted but which through normal delay, inertia or whatever you want to call it, was put off until eventually the purchase was missed entirely.

We notified subscribers of the book selected, described it thoroughly and told them they need not accept it; but if **not**, they must notify us before a given date by using the postage-paid BRE (Business Reply Envelope) we furnished. Otherwise, it would be sent. In other words, they could say "no" to buying any book selected by the judges, but if they didn't say "no" before a given date they were presumed to have said "yes".

Little did we dream this would eventually be attacked by the Federal Trades Commission.

Originally I called it the "inertia plan" because it was thought at the time to be a sales incentive that relieved the subscriber of the job of ordering something he wanted but knew in his heart he would never order if left to his own devices. There was no feeling on our part whatever that inertia meant the dumping of books on unsuspecting people who were just too lazy or too preoccupied to return a card refusing the book offer. Little did we dream this would eventually become known as the "negative option plan" and that it would be attacked by no less a governmental authority than the Federal Trades Commission.

Similar objections or accusations could cast doubt upon any business.

The FTC attacked it and initiated a proceeding for preparing a trade regulation relating to this plan. From the five major objections to the plan, a stranger to advertising, or business, or mainly to mail order procedure would gather that any "of-the-month" club operations would have to automatically be seen as sneaky or crooked. Similar objections or accusations could cast doubt upon any business, bank, publisher, chain store, supermarket or anyone. Mainly the complaint declared that the "of-the-month" sales technique relied substantially on exploiting such human traits as procrastination and forgetfulness. They mentioned centralized collection methods, shortness of time to return the "no" cards, failure to end memberships after receiving cancellations and other infractions which could apply to any business.

Many years after leaving Book-of-the-Month Club I was interviewed by an attorney for the Federal Trades Commission, and to prepare myself I wrote to the largest and most prominent operators of the "of-the-month" clubs for their frank evaluation of the controversial "negative option plan". Here are some of the replies I received.

> There is no doubt in my mind that the (inertia) factor
> has been the life blood of clubs ... without an 'inertia'
> plan book clubs and record clubs as they exist today
> would just not have been possible.

Another said:

> All our studies have shown over and over that the
> basic reason for joining this type of club is the wish
> to get away from having to make a choice in selecting
> a book or record. It is the subscriber who prefers to
> let the experts choose for him knowing that he will

overcome his inertia if he strongly disagrees with the expert's choice. That concept is the backbone of this type of club .... it is the main reason the sales of so-called inertia clubs are higher than when a free choice is given.

One publisher wrote:

> I agree that the 'inertia plan' has been vital to the development of book clubs, record clubs, and all similar mail order propositions. The name 'inertia plan' is certainly the most apt description.

Another comment:

It is the most important factor over a long period of time.

> I can't help feel, since nothing has come along to replace it in all the years since you first put it into operation, that it is the most important factor in keeping up a subscriber's continuing purchase over a long period of time. I believe the whole growth of the mail order 'club' business has been dependent on this 'inertia' principle.

From Canada:

> Your concept of the 'inertia plan' is quite correct. Without this, I do not think any book club would ever have gotten off the ground. Some time ago through error, one of our forms was incorrectly printed, making it necessary for the member to forward it if he wanted the book. It was a minor disaster!

Another from Canada:

> Of course, the plan you describe is the 'inertia plan' and it has been the life blood of all club operations since you initiated it. I am not saying this on the spur of the moment because I have long subscribed to the

'inertia plan' approach and used it with tremendous success.

This excerpt came from a prominent book club advertising expert:

> Certainly the 'inertia' plan as you call it has been the most important factor in book and record club growth. Even record clubs which currently sometimes have a refusal rate as high as 70% still hesitate to abandon it.

So successful has this product of imagination been that during the past years practically every "of-the-month" club has operated on this principle.

They work on the law of averages and thus far the average hasn't been bad.

Yes, the inertia plan can be used successfully if your product will stand repeating. Unlike the sending of unordered merchandise, the terms of sale are clearly stated and a signed order is received. Of course, all automatic shipment plans, whether for books, fruit, neckties, plants, records or what-nots involve strenuous collection methods, but they work on the law of averages and thus far the average has not been bad.

Advertising is a young mind's business, not a young man's business. It isn't how old you are -- it's how bold you are. How resourceful and resilient; how courageous and contagious!

-- Maxwell B. Sackheim

CHAPTER SEVEN

HOW IMAGINATION DEFEATS FAILURE

Finding everything out for ourselves in business is time consuming, painful, expensive, and too frequently, impossible! Therefore, whenever the experience of others is available why not take advantage of it -- adding to, subtracting from or modifying as experience dictates?

When we were tiny children the word we most frequently heard was "DON'T". But despite these sharp warnings we had to learn many things through experiencing them. We learned that fire was hot, that ice was cold, that stairs could hurt, and we learned permanent lessons each time we ignored the parental admonition "don't" and suffered a fall, a burn or scald, or the "tummy ache from eating green apples".

Learning through the experiences of others is an easier way to learn important lessons, and applies as much to failures as it does to successes. Knowing what **not to do** is as important as knowing what **to do**.

In direct mail the successes get around.

It is perfectly natural to adopt, adapt and apply the gimmicks, gadgets and methods that we see over and over again. The artful first paragraphs, the special offer techniques, the value premiums, the double window envelopes or any of the many other successful features of profitable mailings. But we must also learn that fire is hot without getting burned ourselves. In direct mail the successes get around. The failures are "oft interred with their bones".

The most important single reason for the failure of mail order ventures is lack of imagination.

Why are there so many failures in mail selling? The answer is, for the same reasons there are so many failures in the restaurant business or any other line of endeavor, plus a few reasons peculiar to the mail order business. I won't mention such obvious causes as incompetence, indolence, lack of capital and the other liabilities which sound the death knell of many enterprises even before they start. The most important single reason for the failure of mail order ventures is lack of imagination, which means lack of a basic central idea. Just as the reason for outstanding success is the presence of a brilliant, sparkling imagination or whatever you want to call that elusive quality which makes people want what you have to offer.

The lesson we can learn is that failures need not be disastrous. They are to be avoided or minimized by careful testing. Testing, however, will never entirely supplant thinking. Eventually before deciding you may have to gamble on your judgment. The element of the time or season or some other condition may make it necessary for you to mail without testing! Trust yourself. Profit by success and failures of others.

When mailed first class it pulled exactly double, or 22%.

Many years ago we made a mailing to druggists for a trade magazine subscription. The first mailing was addressed to the drugstore owner -- not to the clerk. It contained a letter, a partial list of those who were receiving the magazine free, an order form and return envelope. The significant figure is that when mailed third class it pulled 11%. When mailed first class it pulled exactly double, or 22%.

This was followed up by a second mailing which, when sent first class mail following the original first class mailing, pulled 7%, but when sent first class mail following the original third class mailing pulled 10%, indicating clearly that first class mail was more effective in this instance.

What we learned from these mailings was that first class mail should be carefully tested against third class mail when mailed to druggists, grocers, doctors, lawyers, presidents of corporations, bankers and other business people.

In the areas where heavy mail is likely to be a burden to the addressee, it might be well worthwhile to demand first class attention.

Let me tell you two stories about the American Express Company -- one a success and the other a flop:

It brought in six times the normally expected results!

American Express asked us to prepare a mailing when they were first starting their credit card business. There was nothing new about the format we used -- a letter, a circular, an application and a return envelope. What was startling was the fact that we mailed 10 million without testing - using some 350 lists -- and bringing in six times the normally expected results! We did test one million one page letters against the two page letter and much to the company's surprise the two page letter was considerably better.

Our classic flop!

Our classic flop for American Express was a travel mailing. It offered 238 different European trips at all sorts of prices. The whole thing was wrong -- the basic idea of trying to sell travel directly by mail, the short time between mailing and sailing, the mixture of inquiry and order requests, the inclusion of a credit card ad and application, all made this a hodgepodge and a disaster.

The lesson we learned here was to say "no" when we don't believe wholeheartedly in a plan, a product, or the mailing itself. In other words, test your judgment before you test any mailing!

Mail order advertising has come a long way and claims the right to be measured by its best -- not its worst, by its successes -- not its failures!

The wise copywriter anticipates unspoken objections and answers them before they can be voiced.

-- Jerry Buchanan

CHAPTER EIGHT

MORE QUESTIONS AND ANSWERS

Q. Many firms have problems in keeping their heads above water in the mail order field. Is it becoming more difficult to sell by mail?

In addition, there is the problem of the rate of growth and the ability to keep picking winners.

So much depends upon the merchandise offered and the ability to finance and manage a business until it turns the corner. The mail order way of selling is difficult in proportion to the owner's ability to succeed in these areas. In addition, there is the problem of the rate of growth and the ability to keep picking winners. It is certainly not an easy marketing method regardless of whether the business is a start-up or has been in operation for years. Naturally, the more competition, the tougher it is to get orders -- even if the competition is from beginners.

Q. Should a mail order campaign be undertaken for a new gadget with tremendous one-time sales appeal?

A straight "one shot" proposition doesn't appeal to me.

If the advertising promotion were to be used as a wedge to get retail stores to stock it and push it - yes. Otherwise, it would be far better to stick to its manufacture and turn the mail order selling over to people who know it best -- the catalog houses which have big lists of mail order customers and the "know how" to do it right and fast. Or, if the item has natural repeat possibilities or an automatic repeat plan so the initial cost per order represents an investment in future business, then I would advertise the item. But a straight "one shot" proposition doesn't appeal to me.

Q. Can expensive items be sold successfully by mail order?

You may have to sell terms not price.

Yes, but you may have to sell terms not price, such as "$32.95 down and four equal monthly payments of $29.99". These expensive one-shot deals can enable a manufacturer to dispose of surplus inventory which he might otherwise have to unload at a great sacrifice. By making a virtue of a liability, one can recapture some of the value without having to take the punishment of a job lot sale. Another application of the single-shot, expensive item mail order approach, is to use mail order as a device to get department store and chain store distribution.

Q. Can a low-priced item be sold successfully by mail order?

To accomplish this, two methods may be used.

The most difficult selling job is selling a low priced commodity profitably. To accomplish this, two methods may be used: (1) Invest a huge sum of money on the theory that it will come back with a profit in the form of continual repeat sales; (2) Combine several small units into one large unit so that the margin of profit will allow for a larger expenditure per unit in money, time and effort to secure a customer.

It would be suicide for a chewing gum company to spend millions of dollars advertising the gum in order to sell each customer a single package. The gum companies pay a high price to create a customer knowing that each customer may chew a hundred packages of gum a year.

Every advertising man knows that some small-unit propositions cannot possibly be successfully marketed even if the entire retail price is profit, because the unit is too small and the selling cost is altogether too high. In every line of business there are countless examples which point to the necessity of securing either greater frequency of purchase on small items, or a larger unit of sale by combining several small items. A good example would be in the Gillette razor campaign, where you must buy a plastic bag containing at least 15 razors, all colored blue. The buyer never knows how many times he has used his present razor sitting on the sink counter, so to be safe, he throws away a perfectly sharp razor and selects another from the bag. Soon, it's time to buy another bag full. What would happen if Gillette decided to create five different colors on those little throw-away razors? You guessed it, frequency of sales would drop drastically. But if they did it and then asked a slightly higher price for the color-pack, the world would probably like the new feature.

You can't buy just one pound.

Merchandise of every sort is sold in quantities at a smaller profit per unit than when sold in single units, but the aggregate profit is always greater. If I make a 75 cent profit on a single item, I can well afford to accept a 45 cent profit per item on the sale of a dozen items at once. Consider the pricing policies of the giant warehouse stores. You can get a great price on a pound of butter, but butter is wrapped in packages of three. You can't buy just one pound. This, of course, goes for every item sold in this type of store.

Q. What are the conditions under which it is smarter to shoot for inquiries instead of direct orders?

In a large measure it depends upon the unit of sale. The higher the dollar unit, the more difficult it is to obtain the order direct from an ad or a mailing. Margin of profit is another factor. There is a considerable advantage in getting inquiries on a seasonal item. A list building program can be conducted out of season for timely pin-point follow-up.

Shooting for inquiries is largely a matter of mathematics.

A rose-growing firm does special inquiry promotion in the midwinter for spring selling, and in midsummer for fall follow-up. Shooting for inquiries is largely a matter of mathematics. You must figure out how much it costs to get a name and then what percentage you convert into customers. You may be able to pay $100 or even $500 per thousand names if you can convert a big enough percentage into actual buyers!

Q. Some experts say "don't give 'em a choice - make it easy". Is it wise to use this single offer approach?

It also inspires confidence and actually removes resistance.

When the average prospective buyer is given a choice of fifteen different items, it gives the person the ego-saving satisfaction of being able to say "no" to fourteen of them. This enables buyers to exercise their personal judgment. It also inspires confidence and actually removes resistance. A multiple choice has the additional advantage of offering a special price for a multiple purchase -- thus increasing the dollar amount of the sale.

Q. Traditionally mail order in-print ads are solid with copy. Do these ads pull better than artistic graphic layouts?

The type size can be a factor, as well as the leading between the lines of type.

YES! The old theory that conversation and price are what sell merchandise is still true. The more you have to say about a product in a given space or time, the more reason you give your prospect for buying. Instead of saying "ask the man who owns one" it would be better to say "why we want you to ask the man who owns one". There is no need to deprive the public of the information it needs to make a decision. But still, to answer your question further, the type size can be a factor, as well as the leading between the lines of type, in making a full text page appealing to the eyes. Serif type far out-pulls sans-serif type in a print ad. (This is serif type face -- the same type face used throughout this book), (this is sans-serif type face which is harder on the eyes when read in large amounts. Fine to use for headlines, but never the body copy).

Q. So many experts get involved with testing colors, postage, self-mailers and other variation options. What is the most important factor in designing a direct response campaign?

When all is said and done, I think the OFFER is the most vital part of a mailing. A wonderful offer on ordinary merchandise is better, in my judgment, than a poor or unimaginative offer on good merchandise. Once you've selected your very best offer, build the rest of your campaign around it.

Q. What is an ideal unit sale price for mass mail order mailing?

One had to roll out very big to break even.

There was a time when a loaf of bread sold for a nickel, as did an ice cream cone. You know what you pay for them now. So I can't give you actual dollar amounts because tomorrow they may be out of date again. But for many years, the $1 to $5 asking price was an ideal figure if you were trying to build up a mailing list of buyers in a hurry. But the margin of profit was so slim, one had to roll out very big to break even.

Today, a more realistic asking price might be $12.95 to $19.95 for a book that would retail in the larger bookstore chains for $29.95 to $49.95. The trouble with minimum pricing is that the margin of profit is so small a prohibitive percentage of orders must be secured. It is better to figure backwards on the likely 1½% to 2%, or 3% to 5% of results normally obtained!

Q. Is there any benefit in using odd figures such as $19.98, $22.49, $39.98 instead of round figures like $20, $22.50 or $40.00 ?

The public has been indoctrinated with department store sales appeals. Even the auto makers have taken a tip from the merchants by offering cars at odd prices instead of rounding off the figures. An odd figure creates the illusion of a price reduction or an amount based on actual costs. An even figure seems contrived to make the maximum profit for the seller. The latest wave of off-the-mark pricing has changed the 9¢ figure to a 7¢ one. Thus you ask $87.97 instead of $87.99.

Q. Has the word "free" lost its effectiveness?

That is the most important factor in advertising copy.

The word "free" has not lost its lure but a bargain is better. As an example, I'd rather have a one cent sale (one at the regular price and another for one cent) than to have one at the regular price and one free. Make it believable, make it plausible. That is the most important factor in advertising copy. We found in many instances it is better to offer a tremendous bargain than to make a free offer.

73

We tested offering two books free plus a third book for $2.00. Then we tested offering three books for $2.00. The latter was about 40% better. Usually the word "free" is tied with some kind of an offer. In such instances I recommend a price deal for the whole package. I prefer this even to a one cent sale. Of course, if your offer is an absolutely free one, with no qualifications, by all means offer it that way.

I have also had great success with "free offers" by asking for 10 to 50 cents to help pay postage and packing. When **"free"** results in a let down after the full offer is understood, it can be harmful.

Q. What are the advantages, if any, of "bill me later" as opposed to "cash with order" or "C.O.D."?

It is the best mail order selling device.

The "bill me later" technique lends itself beautifully to automatic renewal of anything that has repeat appeal. It is the best mail order selling device. It batters down suspicion and resistance. It immediately inspires confidence in your offer.

Every device that removes resistance is bound to increase the percentage of orders. From a business point of view, you must balance the increased percentage of response against credit losses; but usually the extra orders more than compensate.

You are saying "we trust you".

When you say "send no money, we'll bill you later" you are saying "we trust you".

Q. How do results compare when cash is required as against C.O.D or open account?

This depends somewhat on the price. Cash is actually far better than C.O.D. in the dollar range. In the $10 range, C.O.D. is about 15% better than cash. We usually ask for some cash in advance on orders above $25, and balance C.O.D; this results in nearly as many orders as all C.O.D. (with many full cash orders). While if the C.O.D. privilege is eliminated, the orders drop 20% or more. The big difference is between open account and cash -- as much as 4 to

1 in favor of open account when the amount is $10 or more. Incidentally, we have done quite a lot of "reservation" mailing. Many years ago on one $5 deal, we asked for $1 in advance, balance when shipment was ready. The "drop-offs" were relatively small because the balance was then only $4. You might want to try this if your proposition fits. Also let me say that losses on open-account deals seldom run over 5% and sometimes as low as a fraction of 1%. The higher the unit, the smaller the percentage of loss as a rule.

Q. How does "safety factor" relate to direct mail?

Direct mail just can't be that scientific.

If you get a 2.5% response on a test, there is no guarantee that you will get the same results on a full run. Direct mail cannot be that scientific. When you mail in large quantities, problems of duplication develop and results frequently fall off. Hence, if you need 2% and you get close to that on a test, you must proceed cautiously because on a larger run your results might easily fall off a half percent. Very rarely will runs exceed the initial test results.

Q. In space advertising it's possible to check the comparative pulling power of copy by using "split runs". How can you approximate this ideal situation in direct mail?

The ideal would be a 1 x 1 sort of the addressed envelopes. (An A-B split). The next best is a "shoe box" sort which alternates clumps of addressed envelopes. The further you get away from this refinement the greater the possibility of error. In any case, I think it's a good idea to double check by spreading each identical group in half again and keying each group separately -- with the identical mailings!

Example: If you were testing 4,000 on copy A and 4,000 on copy B, split group A into 2 lots of 2,000 each with everything identical except the key. Do the same with copy B. If either key on either copy effort varies substantially, something has gone wrong with the sampling selection. If the keys on either copy test pull approximately the same, then you can proceed with some measure of confidence.

Q. How long should an uncovered inquiry be kept in the files?

"There's gold in them thar hills" if you keep working the mine.

My classic answer is "Until he buys, dies, or says *why*". My experience has been that most companies throw their inquiry and ex-customer names away too soon. "There's gold in them thar hills" if you keep working the mine. It's generally the best mailing list you can get. Keep after it and after it and after it. Never mind what some big catalog houses do. They cannot gamble on sending their big catalogs to old names because the loss in undeliverables would eat them up. But you may be able to send a thousand letters or a thousand double postcards at a very reasonable gamble price. One client increased the size of his active mailing list from 400,000 to a million in five years by the simple expedient of constantly hammering his old names. Be absolutely sure before you discard any name in your files regardless of how old. Get some sort of a reply if you possibly can before you give up.

Q. Should one use trick stuff (patented folders, envelopes, premiums, stamps, plastic novelties, coupons, checks, ETC.)?

Cleverness can be a curse.

The answer is yes, however, you must first consider your offer. Will your clever approach add to, or take away from the offer? Cleverness can be a curse. It can attract so much attention to itself as to detract from the offer you are making. All these elements must aid your argument. In fact, they must be intimately tied in with your deal or it may defeat its purpose.

One of our clients found that stamps worked but an allowance check did not. He thinks the stamps conveyed a message while the allowance check was obviously a phony check! Another used a penny pasted on letterheads and asked for the return of the penny when you order! He got pennies back, too! Figure that one out. Use trick stuff when it can be used without being tricky.

Q. Do you believe in celebrity testimonials?

Do not underestimate the intelligence of people. It just is not believable that a movie star has willingly and gratuitously recommended a product. I prefer testimonials from the average "man on the street". They are more believable.

Q. Is it wise to slant ad copy toward current news items?

If your news can be current at the time of mailing, use current news as your point of contact. The trouble with news is that it is apt to change from day to day, from week to week and certainly from month to month. If your appeal is general you are safer in projecting your mailings after your tests are in. Any sales story based on today's news will surely be stale tomorrow, and so will the direct response results.

Q. Are booklets more effective than circulars?

Not according to my experience. Perhaps it is because a booklet looks too formidable, too argumentative. Psychologically it may say to the reader "I dare you to defy or resist me". A circular simply says "here's the deal, take it if you like or not if you don't". It is a quick way, it permits a better display and it is cheaper to print. Booklets may be better for some highly specialized or technical articles or services, particularly if high priced and require a great deal of study, but not for most types of direct mail selling.

Q. Is the dollar savings of using third class bulk mail still worth it?

What they do with it is pretty much up to us.

People like to get mail. They like to throw it away too if it is not interesting. What they do with it is pretty much up to us. The average direct mailer is satisfied if there is 2%, 3%, 5% or 10% in orders. That means he expects at least 90% or more of all pieces to go directly into the trash basket. However, we have found that a third class indicia, and a pasted on address label will cause at least 35% more of your mail to be discarded unopened. Today, with the advent of computers and laser-printing capacities for addressing envelopes and inserting personal names inside the sales letter copy, it is totally foolish to ignore them and try to stay with what worked in direct mail when I was in my younger years.

Q. What months are best for mailings?

Other than strictly seasonal factors such as summer frocks or winter woolens, best results are obtained in January, February, March, July, August, September and October. The worst months are April, May, June, November and December. As a rule it is far better to mail early than it is to try to "hit the nail on the head". It is much easier (and costlier) to be too late than too early.

Apparently January is the month during which gardeners plan, so there is greater interest in catalogs in January when the ground is frozen than during the months closer to planting time. The same thing happens in the fall. July inquiries are bought cheaper than September for all catalogs. The book clubs begin their fall campaigns in the midst of July heat waves and practically end all their selling efforts the first of April. This may not be true of efforts to sell customers but only to sell new prospects.

Watch your climate, whatever it is.

We once made a test of a new product that paid well in September. We decided to hold the mailing up until November when Christmas buying would be in full swing. The November mailing flopped. We should have mailed in September when the climate was right. There may be other "climates" that are peculiar to your business. Do not ignore them. Do not try to force the sale of anything that is not wanted when you are offering it. Watch your climate, whatever it is.

Here's a theoretical example:

If I were a gift fruit shipper (like Harry & David's Fruit-of-the-Month Club in Oregon), I would give tremendous importance to making sales locally to residents and non-residents, especially for shipments to other climates. In every shipment I would distribute printed forms saying "If you know anyone else who might like to hear about our fruit please give us their name and address".

I would put local advertising on my payroll in an effort to lure visitors and residents to my grove or store. Do not say you cannot afford to advertise -- you cannot afford not to.

I would make a deal with hotels, motels, restaurants and shops, where visitors gather, to distribute my circulars or at least invitations to visit my orchard or store. Some method of compensation could be arrived at and kept within your budget.

I would find the names of companies within a reasonable radius which have main offices or branch offices in the north, and circularize my offers through these local offices.

I would try to make every customer a salesman for me.

I would try to make every customer a salesman for me, for what better salesman is there for any company than a satisfied customer?

Offer a half bushel of fruit free to anyone who gets (quantity) orders for you. Enclose half a dozen of your beautiful mouth-watering postcards for customers to send to their friends recommending you and your product.

One very imaginative fruit orchardist inaugurated a plan whereby a customer could "adopt" one tree in the orchard, and actually have his or her name fixed to the trunk. All the fruit from that tree was the customers to keep, sell, or give away. The price of the tree was set high enough that the orchardist made lots of profit, no matter what the "tree owner" did with the fruit.

Tell them you missed them!

I would not be in a hurry to throw old names away unless a customer died or moved and left no address. Tell them you missed them! Tell them all the nice things that happened to you and your groves and your fruit this year. Make them feel guilty for not having reordered lately. Threaten to remove their name from your list unless they send you an order, but do not do it. You will be amazed at how many names you can keep on your list for four or five years, or even longer, profitably even if they do not repeat within the traditional period.

Work your lists to the limit. Begin your Thanksgiving and Christmas mailings early. Make your customers feel you are anxious to do business with them. Offer a special inducement for reservation orders to be shipped later. Do not necessarily ask for money in advance, but bill before shipment if you are concerned about credit.

How is your list divided -- by date of inquiry or last purchase? By amount purchased? Modern methods can pinpoint your message to every select group. Your best customers might be offered a $50 or $100 "drawing account" so to speak, and you can bill them once a month or after Christmas, or next year. Open account is responsible for over a billion dollars worth of credit card business. Make arrangements with American Express and other credit card clubs for charging purchases.

Be extremely careful in the use of outside mailing lists. I think you would lose money if you persisted in mailing to strangers, but if you decide to test outside lists, get all the information you can from list brokers, of which there are many. Offer your own list, however small, in exchange for an equal number of other companies' names.

There are other applications of this device.

Take a close look at some ideas gleaned from other mail order businesses. I'm sure you remember the gummed stamps sent out by the various non-profit fund raising organizations. Undoubtedly the idea of using perforated, gummed stamps in direct mail selling was borrowed from them as an effective stimulant to obtaining results. Books and records particularly, illustrated on gummed stamps, invite readers to make a selection. There are other applications of this device. One year, way back in April or May I received a Christmas card mailing from a company offering a discount for early orders. A different gummed stamp showed what the discount would be if my order was received in May, June, July and so on. I ordered early and used the stamp that earned the biggest discount.

Do you use "riders"? Riders are those little squares at the bottom of coupons or order forms which "trade up" a certain percentage of customers. This "trade up" has been in the form of a discount for cash, or a switch from a cloth bound to a deluxe bound set of books, or from a six months trial subscription to a year or two. There are countless ways to add a little extra to your average order. By using a "rider" it may actually mean the difference between profit and loss.

Silence would certainly have said that.

Some of the largest and most successful mail order operators have used the "yes" or "no" technique. We used it way back in 1922 but it is still effective. There is no reason in the world for anyone to return an order form marked "no". Silence would certainly have said that. But, many actual tests have proved that when you ask for a "yes" or "no" the percentage of "yes" returns is greater than when you do not ask for "no" returns. Maybe somehow, somewhere you can use that gimmick even if only to make them say "no" if they do not want your next catalog instead of letting them go by default.

It may be something completely foreign to your line.

Have you ever offered a self-liquidating premium - something worth $1.00 for your cost of only 49 cents, or a $2.00 value for your cost of 99 cents, or a $5.00 value for your cost of $2.98? All, of course, tied in with certain minimum quantity purchases. It may be something completely foreign to your line. Skirmish around for something grown or manufactured, domestic or imported.

Have you explored the greater possibilities of combination offers? These combinations can increase your average sale. People love "deals".

For years we sent a coupon to all new inquiries, good for 50 cents when applied to a purchase of $5 or more. It is hard to throw 50 cents away, and your average order will be greater than $5. If you cannot afford a 50 cent coupon give them a 25 cent coupon. Call it a "new customer dividend" if you like and say frankly why you are offering it.

With postal rates ever on the increase, have you done as much as you can toward combining your mailing with non-competing products? Are there other items that others will gladly pay to advertise in your mailing -- such as nurserymen do for certain magazine publishers?

Q. Does the extra cost of using color in an ad justify itself?

My long experience has shown that the added expense of color in an ad usually does not pay unless the ad is for food or other items requiring more enhancement. However, with electronic color processing in the state of accelerated advancement in technology, the costs could continue to be reduced. When this happens, the days of effective black and white ads may be over except in the case of classifieds or small display ads. When you can use color printing to effectively deliver the message of your product and company image, I am all for it. Make the most of color pictures that really tell a vivid story. The results may well justify the effort and expense.

Q. Is there any way to offer Gift Certificates so that recipients can send them in for certain items whenever they want them without knowing how much was paid for them?

This can be tricky and can sometimes backfire on you if you have not key-coded the certificate with time-limit dates or value of certificate toward the gift, etc. Never assume the customer will understand your offer. Make it so it cannot possibly be misunderstood. Gift certificates **can be** an effective way to generate more revenue once they are set up correctly.

Q. What's the best way to handle complaints?

"The unspoken objective".   A friend of ours in the gift fruit shipping business anticipates and answers many complaints before they come in! Here is how he does it. With every shipment he includes a broad guarantee and at the same time explains some of the things that can happen to a customer's order. He writes, "To avoid misunderstanding we wish

to call your attention to several special circumstances which are peculiar to the shipment of citrus fruits from Florida". Then he proceeds to enumerate some of the dire things that may cause a complaint -- the color of the fruit, the size of the fruit, the seed in the fruit, the apparent "shortage" due to settling of the fruit in the crate, and the matter of spoilage. These frank answers to possible complaints eliminated most of the correspondence about insignificant matters. And this psychological ploy is what my friend Jerry Buchanan calls "handling the unspoken objection". He says you must anticipate all possible objections that might cause a failure to close or a refund request, and then answer them before they are voiced. Once the prospect voices an objection, it stays in his mind, no matter how well the sales person answers it. But if the objection is anticipated and answered before the prospect or customer voices it, the objection slides by almost unnoticed, and is quickly overlooked.

That's a good sales lesson for you to remember, no matter what you are selling!

Q. Is there a way a company can profit by the "of-the-month-club plan", or "of-the-year club plan" as a gift idea?

YES! I know of several florists who set up automatic deliveries to loved ones on their birthday, anniversary, etc. The purchaser does nothing except pay the bill when due. I'm sure you can come up with something like this for your business.

When we launched Book-of-the-Month Club, subscribers were told if they did not say no before a given date they were presumed to have said yes. Instead of getting 5% to 10% repeat orders, we got 50% to 75%. So successful has this plan been during the past years that practically every "of-the-month" club has operated on the same principle.

Now I have a question that I would like to ask YOU!

Q. How thoroughly do you analyze your results, item by item, charging each item for the space it occupies in a catalog or space ad?

Maybe a little more auditing is in order.

There are many extenuating circumstances which affect your decisions, particularly those pertaining to cost of production and inventory. It might indicate the need for greater change if each item had to pay for its own space. I have a feeling your mailings are pretty well set from year to year almost without regard to profit per item because it's easier to leave them that way than to change. Maybe a little more auditing is in order.

The sculptor St. Gaudens insisted that his students step back a dozen paces from their work every thirty minutes so they could view it from the proper perspective -- and that is what you should do periodically. Take the time to do an overview of your business every so often, to see where you have been and where you are going. Flying blind is only for dare devil stunt pilots.

Good Luck and God Bless
Maxwell B. Sackheim

A Note From the Publisher:

It's not often when you come across a book that contains so much wisdom that it deserves a second, third, and fourth reading.

Well this happens to be one of those books.

While preparing this book for publication, we had the pleasure of reading its content at least ten times. Each time, we learned we had missed many important points of extreme value in previous readings. Maxwell B. Sackheim was a **true genius** in this great field of advertising. His likes may never pass this way again!

Here are what some of the greats in the advertising industry had to say about Maxwell B. Sackheim:

- **Bob Stone,** Chairman of Stone & Adler:
"In every field of endeavor there is at least one man who becomes noted for giant advancements through the medium of unique breakthroughs. Max Sackheim is such a man. He developed new marketing techniques for direct marketing which accrued to the everlasting benefit of all who succeed by printed word."

- **Pete Hoke**, Editor of *Direct Marketing*:
"Maxwell Sackheim is the granddaddy of that rare breed of direct marketing genius who can look at nearly any selling situation, clearly detect and compose its right offer, direct it to the right people at the right time; then know that he's done it by collecting and analyzing concrete results."

- **David Ogilvy,** of Ogilvy & Mather:
"I have learned a lot from Maxwell Sackheim."

- **William Bernbach,** of Doyle, Dane, Bernbach:
  "Maxwell Sackheim beat new and enduring paths into the wilderness of communications. He was a great pioneer."

- **Rosser Reeves,** former Chairman of Ted Bates:
  "For sheer sales power and barehanded accomplishment, Max Sackheim stands alone!"

- **Arthur W. Schultz,** Chairman of Foote, Cone & Belding:
  "Maxwell Sackheim knows how to write advertising that sells and has proved it many times."

- **Stephen J Stuart,** Publisher/Editor of Couponing & Sampling Services Directory; Marketing Director of the Amsterdam Company; Marketing Manager for Mailbag International:
  "After experimenting, creating and developing new mail order techniques, I find myself coming back more often to the tried and true fundamental propositions that Maxwell Sackheim pioneered."

- **Ed Acree,** Wilson & Acres:
  "The name Maxwell Sackheim is synonymous with outstanding results in direct mail advertising. Since the Sackheim legend is true, his place as the 'dean of direct mail' is secure in the history of marketing communications."

Keep this book in a prominent place on your business book shelf. Plan to read it at least seven times to ensure absorption of its entire content.

Compilers: Jerry Buchanan and David Reecher

Billion Dollar Marketing
CONCEPTS AND APPLICATIONS

BOOK TWO

Speeches, Essays,

Articles and Display Ads

from the

Sackheim Archives

Excerpts From the Speech Given by Maxwell Sackheim at the Ninth Annual Direct Mail Day in Chicago 1962.

"I am the field of advertising."

"I am a salesman of goods and services, a marketer of ideas, a reporter, researcher, harbinger of good news. I am known by one name, but I have a thousand faces. I am addressed to people everywhere, and I speak the languages of all. The *sanctum sanctorum* of the mightiest monarch of industry is as open to me as the home of the most modest office clerk. When I speak, the doctor, lawyer, businessman, truck driver and housewife all listen. The whole world is my domain. If I must cross a continent or a hemisphere to deliver my message, I do so. I tell my story in ten words or ten thousand, with a hundred pictures or none. I clothe myself in quiet black and white or many gaudy colors. I deck myself in the flowing style of Victorian times or in streamlined modern garb; thus I am the most flexible, convenient and economical medium of communication available to any enterprise. I am an important force in our nation's economy; I employ millions of Americans full and part-time and I account for billions of dollars of sales each year. I am the showcase of countless businesses and the main sales tool of a myriad of others. I am always your friend and servant, ready to move your goods, sell your services, enlighten your prospects, inform your customers, raise money for your worthy charities - or simply to deliver your message, whatever it is. In the hands of the inefficient, I can fail miserably at my appointed task; but when I am carefully planned, correctly phrased and properly presented by people who know my potential and have watched my experience, I am an effective creator of sales, an efficient purveyor of services and a powerful ambassador of good will. I am Direct Response Advertising ... and proud of it."

"What a challenge that is to direct mail! That's why I hope some of my experiences and some of my memories may be helpful. If in relating them I use the personal pronoun to excess, please forgive me. It is my proudest possession. I have lived with it for nearly 72 years and it has fed, clothed and sheltered me."

"My first advertising job was right here in Chicago in 1905. The agency was Long-Critchfield Corporation and their offices were in the Powers building on Wabash Avenue, where the rear windows overlooked the spacious lawn on Grant Park. One bright snowy winter day I watched a number of boys playing tag in the park below, and I noticed that their footprints made a clear and distinct pattern in the snow. After the boys left, and the falling snow had obliterated their tracks, I sneaked out of the office, went to the park, and tramped a huge trademark of our company in the snow."

"My boss happened to be looking out the window and saw me doing it. When I got back to the office he sent for me and raised my salary from $3 to $3.50 per week."

"That was my first advertising experience. Since that time in 1905 I've spent or have been responsible for spending more than 250 million dollars in advertising."

A few words about selling by mail

No wonder the mail order people were scared.

"It was started in 1870 by Montgomery Wards. Sears Roebuck followed, and in 1913 did about $250,000,000, almost every dollar of it by mail. Around 1915, some of their top men were greatly concerned about the future of the mail order business because the automobile enabled people to shop in stores nearby. Then came good roads and even faster travel to town; and the universal use of the telephone made it possible to order without writing a letter or driving to the store at all! Of course, time for reading, which is indispensable to the success of the mail order business, almost vanished when these and other attractions and distractions usurped a good part of our 24 hours per day. There was no inflation so far as our allotment of time was concerned. No wonder the mail-order people were scared."

"But what happened? In spite of automobiles, telephones, movies, chain stores, supermarkets, enormous retail outlets and more recently the demands of radio and television, the mail order business became greater than it was in the horse-and-buggy days. According to some estimates, Sears' mail order volume last year [1961] was about 10% of their total, or about $450,000,000."

"Sears and Wards do more business by mail now than they did when buying by mail was almost a necessity. Not only is it true of Wards and Sears, but of Spiegels, Aldens, plus a host of Johnny-come-latelys like Book-of-the-Month-Club, Columbia Record Club, *Literary Guild*, Harry and David's Fruit-of-the-Month-Club and many of our largest magazines like *Time, Life, The Saturday Evening Post, Cosmopolitan*, and thousands upon thousands of other large and small enterprises which deal almost entirely by mail. And why not? Buying by mail is economical, convenient, safe; it avoids the crush of crowds, eliminates parking problems, enables new enterprises to start small without long-term obligations."

That elusive quality which makes people want what you have to offer.

"These, plus the many other good reasons for buying and selling by mail give rise to the question, 'why are there so many failures in mail selling?' The answer is for the same reasons there are so many failures in the restaurant business or any other line of endeavor, plus a few reasons peculiar to the mail order business. I won't mention such obvious causes as incompetence, indolence, lack of capital and the other liabilities which sound the death knell of many enterprises even before they start. The most important single reason for the failure of mail-order ventures is lack of imagination, which means lack of a basic central idea ... just as the reason for outstanding success is the presence of a brilliant, sparkling imagination or whatever you want to call that elusive quality which makes people want what you have to offer."

10,862 Eggs in One Month

"Now let's see how IMAGINATION works. Some of you may remember the old Gundlach advertising agency here. E.T. Gundlach was one of the early mail order advertising pioneers. One of his accounts was E.J. Reefer of Kansas City, who was advertising a tonic intended to make hens lay more eggs. Gundlach's headlines were '10,862 Eggs in One Month.' '4,685 Eggs Last Week' etc. In the body of the ad he quoted some details and revealed the number of hens involved so the number of eggs meant something. The price of the tonic was $1 a package, cash in advance."

So many of these ads appeared, we knew they must have been successful.

"Attracted by the tremendous volume of advertising Reefer was doing, competition soon appeared. Among these competitors were Mr. & Mrs. Carswell, also from Kansas City. Ruthrauff & Ryan's Chicago office got the Carswell account and we used Bessie Carswell as our personality to tell the story of increased egg production - because women were the chicken raisers on the farms. Then, instead of asking for the dollar in advance we borrowed an idea from Walter Field, a large Chicago mail order operator in the dress business. Practically every Walter Field ad was headed, 'Send No Money.' So many of these ads appeared, we knew they must have been successful. So we offered Carswell's hen tonic on a 'send no money' basis - pay the postman when the package arrives - and the Carswell campaign was hugely successful. Were we original? No. We just put two and two together and out came four! So did Walter Field, I guess, because Richard W. Sears advertised 'Send No Money' as far back as 1898!"

"In 1914 Harry Scherman and I published Little Leather Library immortal classics bound in genuine leather and sold at 25 cents each through stores, with only moderate success. After struggling with this idea for five years we decided to bind the books in imitation leather and offer them at 10 cents each - by mail. At that time $2.98 was a popular mail order price so we made up a set of 30 titles and offered them at that price. What was our clincher - SEND NO MONEY! Pay the postman on arrival. We sold about

40,000,000 of these classics, practically all by mail. It was quite a jump from dresses to egg tonic to masterpieces of literature - but we made it!"

This DM letter has been reprinted on the next page.

"One of our direct mail efforts included a letter which went something like this: 'You don't know me from Adam, but I understand you are a book-lover; if so, how much would you guess 30 books, bound in the material enclosed, should sell for, to be a sensational bargain?'"

Directly following the letter is the ad that capitalized on the customers high guesses.

"The letter listed the titles, enclosed a sample of the material, gave some other details and requested the reader to make a note of his guess; then to open the sealed envelope enclosed, and see what the actual price was. You can imagine the impact of the $2.98 price if the reader guessed that $5, $7.50, $10 or as much as $50 would be a bargain price. The order form was a Government post card which requested a yes or a no answer, and provided a space for the customer's guess! We mailed millions of those letters."

"When the sale of sets slowed down, we worked out a plan to send a book each week for a year on a subscription basis, for $5, and called it, Book-of-the-Week Club - but it never got off the ground. Instead, we started a company called National Music Lovers which sold phonograph records by mail. As in book publishing, we concentrated on the classics: Grand opera selections, symphonies, spirituals, folk songs and so on. Finally, we offered a set of popular music, including a song called, 'Yes, We Have No Bananas.' Our sales increased to a million dollars annually until radio knocked the bottom out of the record business. Then our thoughts returned to books. We recalled our Book-of-the Week thinking and combined our idea of selling books by subscription, with our experience in selling popular records as against classics; and that was the beginning of Book-of-the-Month Club."

NEW YORK, N.Y.

Dear Friend:

You don't know me from Adam, but I have been
told that you are a book-lover, that you have bought
good books in the past, and that apparently you like
to have them around you.

If this is so, you are unquestionably a
person of taste and judgment, and you know what good
books should sell for--you are able to measure not only
their cultural value, but their intrinsic worth in
dollars and cents.

What, then, do you think a library of <u>thirty</u>
of the world's masterpieces, bound in a rich and beautiful cover like the sample enclosed, should sell for?

How much, in other words, would you personally be willing to pay for thirty such books, <u>each
one complete,</u> <u>each one an acknowledged masterpiece?</u>

Keep in mind that volumes like these are not
only an adornment to the library table; but the size
makes them very convenient to carry with you to read
while traveling.

I suggest that you compare this binding
with other books in your library; estimate what <u>thirty</u>
such books should reasonably sell for - AND THEN OPEN
THE ENCLOSED SEALED ENVELOPE AND SEE HOW CLOSE YOUR
GUESS IS TO THE ACTUAL COST.

I shall be very much interested to know
<u>what your first guess was</u> and will appreciate it if you
will fill in the card (which is also enclosed in the
sealed envelope) giving me this information.

Thanking you in advance for this courtesy.

Cordially yours,

Harry Scherman

Why Was Their *Average* Guess Six Times The Actual Price?

Here is a bargain in books that some book-lovers estimated was worth as high as THIRTY times the actual price; the AVERAGE of 884 estimates, made by intelligent book-lovers, was SIX TIMES the price. NOT A SINGLE GUESS was too LOW. What would be YOUR guess?

A *value that seems too good to be true*

IF you are a book-lover, if you like to have good books around you, you unquestionably know what good books should sell for. Here, then, is the new de luxe edition of a set of World's Masterpieces—the value of which we ask you to estimate. You will find in this set the finest works of such immortal authors as:

Kipling	Elizabeth	Irving
Shaw	Browning	Plato
Barrie	Dumas	Poe
Balzac	Lamb	Turgenev
Ibsen	Whitman	Longfellow
Wilde	Whittier	Tennyson
Maeterlinck	Dante	Elbert Hubbard
Yeats	Shakespeare	James Allen
Browning	Emerson	Thomas Moore

Each one of these inspiring books is complete; they are NOT extracts.

In making your estimate of their value, be guided by these facts. There are almost 3,000 pages in the set. The binding is a beautiful replica of hand-tooled leather, tinted in an antique copper and green. The paper is the same as that used in books usually selling for $1.50 to $2.00 per volume. The type is clear and easy to read. These volumes are pocket-size; they can be carried conveniently in a pocket wherever you go, for spare-time reading while traveling.

Samples of these books were sent to 884 book-lovers, people who owned libraries. We asked them to guess what this set of 30 books was worth. Here are

What 884 Book-lovers Guessed

140	estimated from	$4.50	to $9.50
132	"	10.00	
288	"	"	14.00 to 15.00
71	"	"	16.00 to 20.00
99	"	"	21.00 to 25.00
115	"	"	30.00
34	"	"	45.00 to 60.00
5	"	"	90.00 to 100.00

their estimates (shown in the panel), AFTER EXAMINING A SAMPLE. The signed estimates are on file in our office for inspection.

Please make *your* guess now—write it, if you will, on the margin of this page. *Our price is quoted in the coupon.* Then compare your estimate with our price.

How it can be done

Please note carefully that the price shown in the coupon is ALL YOU PAY FOR THE ENTIRE THIRTY VOLUMES. This publication would not allow us to advertise here unless every statement we made were true.

There is no secret as to how this extraordinary offer can be made. These books are printed in editions of nearly a MILLION at a time. That is the whole story—"quantity production." Close to THIRTY MILLION of these volumes have already been purchased.

Send no money

It is impossible in the printed page to do justice to the beauty and character of these books. You must SEE them—so we ask you to let us send you a set for examination. You need not send any money now. Simply mail the coupon or write a postal card or letter. When the books arrive pay the postman, then examine the set. Ask some of your friends to guess what these books are worth. Decide in your own mind their value. If you have the slightest doubt of your bargain, return them any time within 30 days and your money will be refunded at once without question or quibble.

ROBERT K. HAAS, Inc., Publishers
(Formerly Little Leather Library Corporation)

218 West 40th St.   Dept. 1210   New York, N. Y.

Illustration above is slightly reduced from actual size

How Book-of the Month Devised 'Inertia Plan'

Something had to be done.

"Here's some history about that enterprise. At first, Book-of-the-Month Club subscribers automatically received the selection of the judges, with the privilege of returning it if it was not satisfactory. Well, books seemed to come back by the carload! Something had to be done. We knew we couldn't afford to notify subscribers in the usual way, in advance, and ask them to order the Book-of-the-Month if they wanted it. All we could hope for on this plan would be a return of 2% or 5% or at most 10%. What a waste of money and time - if we could survive at all!"

"Imagination came into play. Why not notify subscribers of the book selected, describe it thoroughly, and tell them they need not accept it - but if not they must notify us before a given date; otherwise, it would be sent. In other words they could say no about buying any book selected by the judges, but if they didn't say no before a given date they were presumed to have said yes."

"So successful has this product of imagination been that during the past 35 years practically every book-of-the-month club has operated on this principle."

Other troubles ruined this effort.

"Back in 1947 we tested this technique with *47 Magazine*. Through direct mail and space advertising we quickly obtained 80,000 subscribers at $4 each. We did this by offering a free sample copy with the understanding that a year's subscription would be entered unless the reservation was cancelled after reading the free copy. Collections were about 90% when the bills were sent out for annual subscriptions. Other troubles ruined this effort, notably an ill-advised newsstand campaign plus a rapidly deteriorating editorial content of the magazine itself. Incidentally, had *47 Magazine* carried advertising as *Reader's Digest* now does, it might have survived."

"One of the most successful enterprises I was fortunate to be involved with was a company selling vitamins by mail, also on the 'inertia plan.' Many tests were made to discover the most profitable

Ad featured on next page.

sales policy. They offered the first month's supply free; for 10 cents, also for 25 cents, and also for $1. Every offer specified that an automatic monthly shipment would follow unless cancellation was received within a given time. The plan that produced a $10,000,000 annual volume was the 25 cent introductory price, and the automatic shipment of additional packages at the full regular price."

"For many years this automatic ordering procedure has been suggested as a method of handling magazine subscriptions and renewals. Why not sell them on a t.f.n. (till further notice) basis? The subscriber is then billed automatically once a year, until he cancels. I understand several magazines are now testing this idea. Its success, or failure, I predict, will depend on how the original sale is made, and the renewal procedure."

"Here is another book club story: A book club offered a certain well known best seller free - if you agreed to purchase four additional books during the year. Results were satisfactory as long as the book was in demand. After a few months, if the book ceased to be a best seller, the ads stopped pulling. On a number of occasions no best seller was available to the club. They then offered a choice of any one of four books free for joining, and results improved."

"Further improvement came when a choice of any one of six books was offered. Results continued to improve as more books to choose from were added and as more variations of offers were presented. When one book was offered free for joining, you were entitled to a free bonus book after your fourth purchase."

Although the deal was basically the same, results improved substantially.

"The offer was then changed to two books free when you joined - the first bonus book being given to you in advance for agreeing to purchase four. Although the deal was basically the same, results improved substantially. Later the offer was changed to two books free provided you immediately bought your first book at the regular club price and agreed to purchase three more. (Mathematically that too was the same offer, yet results again improved).

Then instead of two books free and one for $2, the offer was changed to 'Three Books for $2,' which also was identically the same as 'Two Books Free and a third for $2.' And again, results improved. I haven't the slightest idea how you can apply this, except to realize that sometimes a bargain is better than the word 'free.' In any event, it again points to the importance of IMAGINATION in advertising."

Ad Without Picture Pulls Traffic

"We have a lot of builders in Florida. One of them, a friend of ours, put up a model house and was anxious to draw good prospects to see it. He tried several regular ads, showing a picture of the house, describing its main features, quoting its price, and generally making the usual claims. On a Sunday, if it was a nice day, about a dozen people would come in response to that approach."

"I changed the ad, and deliberately omitted the picture of the house; the copy was long, and written in the first person. It described every detail of the house minutely, even the tiny cook-book-shelf in the kitchen. The headline I used was:"

**"Am I Crazy To Sell
This House For Only $13,250?"**

We avoided the feeling of it being "just another house."

"The copy explained why no picture was shown - you had to see this house to believe it, and so on. The Sunday the ad appeared, 250 people came to see the house, and before the week was over, another hundred came. By not showing a picture of the house and by describing it in such detail we may have avoided the feeling of it being 'just another house'."

Catalogs - Should You Sell Them or Give Them Away?

Inquiry costs were affected, but closures were vastly improved.

"The question often comes up as to whether to offer a catalog free, or to charge 25 cents to $1.50. My experience has demonstrated that it is best to offer the catalog free. However, if the conversions are too small to justify, it may be well to qualify inquiries by asking an extra question or two in a coupon or reply card, such as 'give name of nearest dealer; or number in family; age if under 21; or a telephone number;' or any one of dozens of other requests for information. A technical school which formerly sent its salesmen on many wild goose chases because of poor quality inquiries included this phrase in their copy: 'Our representatives do not have time to visit the merely curious but will be glad to call on you if you are sincerely interested.' Inquiry costs were affected, but closures were vastly improved."

Perhaps this type of candor might be more productive to insurance companies.

"In an issue of the *New York Times* the story was told of a direct mail campaign conducted by a mutual fund sales agency. The prospects were promised nothing except full information as to the best mutual fund for them to invest in, depending upon each person's objective. Out of a 2,000 mailing, which incidentally mentioned $10,000 as the minimum amount in which the fund was interested, 20 leads came in, or 1%. Of these, 18 agreed to see a salesman, after which ten invested in funds in amounts ranging from $4,000 to over $50,000. Perhaps this type of candor might be more productive to insurance companies and others who promise a bribe of a leather covered memorandum book if you return the card with your birth date or other desired information."

Pipe ad featured next page.

"One of our most successful direct mail campaigns was for a smoking pipe which sold for $2. It was a good pipe - so good that money back was offered if it wasn't completely satisfactory - but the customer was asked to break the pipe and return the pieces, if a refund was requested. Very few broken pipes came back!"

If you have a cure for some of them, price may not matter much.

"IMAGINATION can offset price disadvantages. Prices in convenience stores are higher than supermarkets, but they render a service which on many occasions is more important than price. If you've ever run out of cigarettes after 10 p.m., you know what I mean. Well, there are many other symptoms comparable to running out of cigarettes after 10 p.m. and if you have a cure for some of them, price may not matter much."

WHY I OFFER YOU THIS NEW KIND OF PIPE FOR 25¢

If you are an old-time pipe smoker, I know how skeptical you are about new pipe inventions. So, before expecting you to buy one of my regular genuine imported briar SANATON pipes, I am offering you this DEMONSTRATOR for only 25c. It is made exactly the same as my genuine imported briar pipes except that the wood isn't briar—but it will serve the purpose of proving to you that the unique SANATON NON-CONDENSING and EASY CLEANING features give you the driest, sweetest, coolest, and cleanest smoke you ever enjoyed from *any* pipe, regardless of name, make, or price! I'm gambling that if my "demonstrator" does this, you will want one of my better grades at $3.50 to $5.00. If not, well, you're out two bits—and I've just kidded myself!

DR. J. C. SHOTTON
Prominent Cleveland, Ohio, dentist—inventor of one of the first welding rods—inventor of the "fish-gun," and many other devices. Considered by all who know him to be an outstanding inventive genius.

Here's what this "demonstrator" must PROVE TO YOU!

Most pipes, in some way or another, are designed to catch and hold "goo." They are equipped with tubes, traps, filters, baffles, and gadgets of all kinds. But, according to Dr. J. S. Shotton, a prominent Cleveland, Ohio, dentist, the *principle* of catching and trapping "goo" is all wrong. So, inventive-minded, he designed and patented a pipe in which the basic idea was to eliminate the *cause* of "goo!"

As Dr. Shotton figured it, moisture is formed in a pipe by *condensation*—just as it is formed on the outside of a pitcher of ice water in a warm room. That's because, as warm air is cooled, it deposits its excess of moisture on a cooler surface.

In the ordinary pipe, as you know, the tubes, filters, baffles, etc., are placed in the *stem*—and condensation takes place because these metal gadgets are colder than the smoke which is drawn through the pipe. It's as inevitable as the formation of fog on a windshield, or frost on the lawn on a cool morning. So—what happens in the ordinary pipe is that the gadgets which are intended to catch "goo" actually help to cause it! And there's no need to tell you that smoke passing over this strong-smelling "goo" absorbs its strength, odor, and bitterness, just as fresh air passing over a stockyards becomes foul and contaminated!

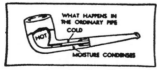

WHAT HAPPENS IN THE ORDINARY PIPE
HOT / COLD
MOISTURE CONDENSES

Now, what did Dr. Shotton do? Well, instead of placing a catch-all gadget in the *stem*, he placed a small slotted tube at the bottom of the *bowl* in his new pipe. This tube acts as a NON-condenser for, as you light this pipe, the tube warms up—and there's no cold surface for moisture to gather on!

It's as simple as that! But the result of such a simple idea is the driest, coolest, sweetest, and cleanest smoke you ever enjoyed!

Dr. Shotton went a step further. He extended the non-condenser tube

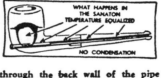

WHAT HAPPENS IN THE SANATON
TEMPERATURE EQUALIZED
NO CONDENSATION

through the back wall of the pipe and attached a tiny removable screw—so whenever you want to clean out the *tar* which results from tobacco combustion, you just remove the screw and run a regular pipe cleaner clean through from end to end—just like cleaning a gun!

Dr. Shotton's non-condensing Sanaton is now being enjoyed by nearly 100,000 pipe smokers—all of whom bought it after *trying* it! Their letters of praise are so enthusiastic you would think the writers are all my relatives! Some are from fellows who have been smoking pipes for 30, 40, and even 50 years. Some are from collectors who say they have 50 to 200 pipes and like the Sanaton better than all the rest put together!

Well, that's the story—except this. I don't expect you to buy my regular *imported briar* Sanaton until you try out the non-condensing and easy-cleaning *principle*. So I've had these *demonstrators* made up of domestic wood. They are easily worth a dollar or maybe a dollar and a half. I'll send you one for only 25c, if you will let me send you a regular imported briar Sanaton after you've tried the demonstrator—provided you like it! You will surely want a *genuine imported briar* Sanaton if the demonstrator is all I say it is, so I'll reserve one for you when I send your demonstrator. Then, in two weeks, if I don't hear from you, I'll send the genuine imported briar Sanaton and you can pay for it when it arrives. The small sizes are $3.50, medium sizes $4.25, and the large sizes are $5.00. But—if you don't like the way my Sanaton *demonstrator* smokes—if you don't find it to be the driest, cleanest, sweetest, and coolest smoke you ever had, just tell me so on the postcard supplied for

that purpose, and I'll cancel your reservation.

I think this is the swellest way in the world to get you to try a Sanaton. You gamble two-bits—that's all—to try a new pipe invention that may or may not please you. On the other hand, I lose money on every 25c demonstrator I sell—so I must have confidence in their ability to sell my regular genuine imported briar Sanatons.

I have only a few thousand 25c "demonstrators" on hand. Under present conditions I don't know when I will get more. I expect a rush of orders from this ad, because these days any kind of pipe is worth a lot more than a quarter. So, if you want to try one of these Sanaton demonstrators on this offer, mail the coupon below, with 25c, right now, before you forget. (Only one to a customer, please.) Thanks.

Mark Foster, Dept. A,
257 Fourth Ave., New York 10, N. Y.

CLEANS LIKE A GUN—STRAIGHT THROUGH FROM END TO END

"Some time ago a publisher was about to put out a very fine cookbook. He was greatly disturbed because his costs would compel him to establish a retail price of $5.00 and he was afraid this would price his book out of the market. It was suggested that he price himself out of the market at $7.50 instead of $5.00 and spend the extra $2.50 in promotion. It became the most successful book he published in years!"

The new price just looked cheaper and customers flocked to save money!

"I remember an item in the *Wall Street Journal* which told about a chain store where dog food was regularly sold at 31 cents for two cans. One day a sign was displayed, offering three cans for 49 cents. The new price was 16 1/3 cent per can, while the old price was 15 1/2 cents per can. The new price just looked cheaper and customers flocked to save money!"

"When we planned the American Express Co.'s credit card campaign, we recommended that the price be made $6.00 per year, instead of $5.00, which Diners' Club was charging. In about two months we mailed 10,000,000 pieces and by the end of the first year they had sold about 800,000 credit cards. That extra dollar could have paid for the 10,000,000 mailing at $80 per thousand. Since then the price of both credit cards has been increased to $8.00 with practically no reduction in membership."

"Another fascinating product of IMAGINATION in advertising is the direct mail campaign conducted by *Reader's Digest* for the renewal of gift subscriptions. Each year they circularize donors, enclosing the names of those to whom subscriptions were given the previous year. All the donor has to do is check the list, eliminating such names as he does not wish to renew, and adding any new names he desires. Five letters were used. We thought we could do as well with four, and save them about 100,000 a year, but the test didn't work that way. The next year we decided to go the other way, and prepare six mailings, one of which was to go out after Christmas. This, too, didn't work out. But two of these letters were made part of the series of five. Something like this might work for you."

"Every great advertising and direct mail campaign is the product of someone's IMAGINATION. Not many years ago oranges were eaten. Now people drink 50 times as many. The story of vitamins in tomato juice placed tomatoes in millions of glasses instead of only on salad plates. Liver that the butcher used to give us for our cats now sells for as much as steak because we learned it was the enemy of anemia. When it was emphasized that flowers were wonderful messengers of our sentiments, we really began to 'say it with Flowers.' Raisins, we were told, provide iron for our blood, and the sale of raisins soared. Lemon juice is good for colds - and lemons are best sellers in supermarkets. Spinach is still spinach to me but the creator of Popeye made kids love it. When Listerine became a cure for halitosis, its sales multiplied."

"I leave you with this sad story. Perhaps you can find a moral, or at least a worthwhile warning in it somewhere."

They must be where the Jordans are, "Somewhere West of Laramie."

"In 1904, there were 121 companies in the U.S. making or assembling automobiles. How many are there today? Where are the Packards, Pierce Arrows, Wintons, Hudsons, Hupmobiles, Peerlesses, Paiges, Locomobiles, Franklins, Overlands, yes and even the Edsels and Henry J's. They must be where the Jordans are, 'Somewhere West of Laramie.' Ask the man who owns one, if you can find him. I'm sure these products were amply financed, well managed, adequately advertised and properly priced. Somewhere *East* of Laramie they failed to capture the public's imagination, maybe because they didn't use enough of their own."

There is no substitute for IMAGINATION. A man with fire in his head can write a torch song for even the dullest product.   Add a sales manager with fire in his belly and you have a great conflagration.

-- Maxwell B. Sackheim

B Y O B

By Maxwell Sackheim
Featured in the June 1975 issue of *The Copy Cornucopia*

I once wrote an ad for an investment advisor. The headline was "If You're So Smart About Investments Why Aren't You a Millionaire?"

The ad never ran because my client thought it guaranteed (predicted) the result of his future stock market advice. Indeed it is against the law to refer to any past performance figures unless quickly and emphatically followed by a clear "disclaimer" to the effect that the past is no indication of what will occur in the future.

However, by going through a personal experience, at one's own risk, one can explain the procedure and process of thinking so that it can be passed along to others.

One of the oldest expressions in our school-day copy books was: **"Experience is the best teacher."**

The gamble is all in our favor.

Thus we should gain actual experience as soon in our advertising careers as we can, and do it as carefully as we will permit. If we lose, it will, at least, be our own cash, not a client's! And we will not feel it necessary to apologize to anyone if our judgment is faulty. On the other hand, if our idea pays, we will have gained, not only profitable advertising experience but perhaps in having started a money-making business of our own, whether in mail order or over-the-counter! The gamble is all in our favor.

I think any advertising man can learn more operating his own business.

When Harry Scherman and I first met at J. Walter Thompson way back in 1914, we decided we would go into some kind of business of our own and started Little Leather Library on a moonlight basis. Later we started Sackheim & Scherman Advertising Agency and developed Book-of-the-Month Club, also more or less on a moonlight basis, in addition to running our advertising agency. I think any advertising man can learn more operating his own business than from making mistakes or creating success for someone else. A part of his income should be invested at his own risk.

I am sure there is no experience more worthwhile than that which comes out or goes into one's own pocket. There are countless examples, the first one of which I can recall was old man Erickson, of McCann Erickson, who also owned the New-Skin Company, and of course, J. Walter Thompson himself, who owned Beecham's Pills and one or two other patent medicines which came from England. Other advertising men who delved into enterprises outside of their own agencies were Albert Lasker, who owned substantial interests in Pepsodent. Wibur Ruthrauff and Fritz Ryan, who owned all of the Madam X Girdle Company, Dr. Cristian, one of the early food faddists, and several others. I believe sincerely every advertising man, especially if in the direct response field, should have a sideline of his own where he will have to make all the decisions including management, financing, copy, etc.

Perhaps that is why there is so many in-house agencies now.

When advertising agency recognition was something sacred and exclusive it was not customary for any agency to 'own' its accounts. There were very few "house agencies." I recall in the early 1900's when Long-Critchfield did the advertising for International Harvester Company, the farm publications paid little attention to news items sent out by the Harvester Company, but when the ad agency sent news items out they were much more favorably acted upon by these same farm publications! Long-Critchfield lost the account and IHC placed their business direct -- after which the farm publications were much more generous with their Harvester Company public relations releases! Perhaps that is why there is so many in-house agencies now -- but I believe the trend should be reversed and there should be many more in-house clients now!

Every day new products are being perfected and their inventors or producers know little or nothing about how to advertise them. They know little or nothing about testing, about attracting favorable attention, about maintaining interests, assuring conviction, inducing action. The average advertising man, particularly in the direct response field sees only a good product, a good margin of profit, good repeat possibility, and good management to start and build up his own "experimental laboratory" where he can do as he pleases and thinks best. He already has the magic ingredient of sales ability instead of working exclusively for a fee or commission, losing accounts, struggling to get replacements, making fortunes for others if his efforts are good or being fired if someone else comes along with a "better idea".

He already has the magic ingredient of sales ability.

During my long experience I have owned or held substantial interests in such enterprises as a rowing machine (which flopped because it had no "repeat" value), a farm supply firm (which went broke two years after I left, because it tried to compete with Sears and Wards in the retail store field), a smoking pipe business (which went up in smoke because it too did not repeat). And during this time I was learning certain principles of failure and a few basic requirements for success in any business.

Who knows--you may even strike it rich!

Make up your own mind then, to learn what to do at your own financial risk -- even if limited to some very inexpensive classified ads -- instead of having to experiment with client's money. Who knows -- you may even strike it rich! I DID! Lasker did! Thompson did! And maybe you are doing it right now!

BYOB may mean bring your own bottle to some ad guys but it meant be your own boss, to me!

If your product and your offer are right, your copy almost writes itself.

-- Maxwell B. Sackheim

Maxwell Sackheim's Acceptance Speech at the New York Copywriters Hall of Fame Awards

October 23, 1975

"Mr. Chairman, Members of the Copy Club, and Guests:"

"I am particularly grateful for having been invited to participate in this program because at my age I will not have many more opportunities to brag about my hitherto carefully guarded secrets of creating direct response copy. This year, 1975, marks my 85th birthday and my 70th year in the business of advertising -- practically every one of which was spent in the field of direct mail, direct response, direct marketing, or whatever other name you may wish to designate your favorite mail order interest."

"Way back in 1905 I tried to imitate the copywriters at the old Long-Critchfield Advertising Agency in Chicago. I didn't have the nerve to show any of them my early efforts but I exposed my ads to a pet pigeon by placing them on the back doorstep of our home. If my pigeon approved he would leave them alone, if not, he would express his displeasure in his own characteristic bird-like fashion!"

I knew it must have hit the bull's-eye of the sales target.

"Soon thereafter I adopted another method of producing direct response advertising. It seems that while driving through a small town in Russia, a pompous army officer observed the side of a wooden structure painted with many targets. In the center of each was the usual bull's-eye, and in the center of every bull's-eye was a bullet hole. The officer was amazed, and stopped to inquire about the sharp-shooter who seemed to never miss. When told he was a 12 year old boy, he insisted the boy be brought before him. 'Oh,' he said, 'I never miss the bull's-eye from any distance because, you see, I shoot first and wherever the bullet strikes I paint the target around it.' In my early days -- and many times during the past 70 years -- I still wrote direct response copy by this method of 'second-guessing.' Whenever I saw an ad repeated again and again, I knew it must have hit the bull's-eye of the sales target and I tried to copy it or adapt it to whatever I was advertising."

What was left , in many instances, was a good job.

"Another method I used was that of the sculptor who never took a lesson in his life but who produced wonderful finished statues. When asked how he did such a fine job of carving elephants out of blocks of granite, he said, 'I look at the block and whatever doesn't look like an elephant I chip off -- and what's left looks like an elephant!' I did something like that in preparing my copy. What didn't look and sound convincing I cut out -- and what was left, in many instances, was a good job."

"I also learned much by observing and listening to others -- like the Chinese laundryman who said his name was Ole Olsen. When asked how he got a name like that he explained it was an official name given to him by the U.S. Government. When they arrived at the immigration office the immigration official asked each entrant his name. The fellow ahead of the laundryman said his name was Ole Olsen. When the Chinaman was asked his name, he said 'Sam Ting' -- and he's been Ole Olsen ever since. I've followed good copywriters for so many years I'm surprised my name isn't Claude Hopkins, John Kennedy, or any name previously elected to the Copywriters Hall of Fame!"

"The best advice I received, however, came from the story I heard about the fellow standing on the corner of Fifth Avenue and Fifty-Seventh Street with a battered old violin case under his arm. A young man approached him and said, 'Excuse me, Sir, but can you tell me how to get to Carnegie Hall?' 'Certainly', came the reply, **'practice, practice, practice!'** And that's what I've been doing since those days in 1905. I've been practicing, practicing, practicing! I intend to keep on practicing. The lesson we must all learn is -- it's never too late. Here are a few examples of what some folks did long after they were supposed to have been through:"

"Benjamin Franklin went to France to serve his country at 72, and wrote his autobiography when he was over 80."

"Verdi at 74 produced his masterpiece OTHELLO, at 80 FALSTAFF, and at 85, the famous AVE MARIA."

"Cato at 80 began the study of Greek."

"Michelangelo painted the ceiling of the Sistine Chapel (on his back, on a scaffold) when he was nearly 90."

"Titian at 98 painted his historic picture of the Battle of Lepanto."

"Goethe completed FAUST when he was over 80."

"So, you see growing old is only a state of mind -- brought on by gray hairs, dentures, wrinkles, big belly, short breath and an all-over feeling of being constantly and totally pooped!"

"Finally, when you feel that old age is catching up with you, remember the lesson in this wonderful anonymous Prayer For The Aging:"

"Lord, thou knowest better than myself that I am getting older and will some day be old."

"Keep me from getting talkative, and particularly from the fatal habit of thinking that I must say something on every subject and on every occasion."

"Release me from the craving to straighten out everybody's affairs."

"Make me thoughtful - but not moody, helpful - but not bossy."

"Keep my mind from the recital of endless details, give me wings to get to the point."

"Seal my lips on my aches and pains. They are increasing, and my love of rehearsing them is becoming sweeter as the years go by."

"I ask for grace enough to listen to the tales of others' pains. Help to endure them in patience."

"Teach me the glorious lesson that occasionally it is possible that I may be mistaken."

"Keep me reasonably sweet. I do not want to be a saint -- some of them are so hard to live with -- but a sour old man is one of the crowning works of the devil."

"Give me the ability to see good things in unexpected places and talents in unexpected people. Give me the grace to tell them so."

"Help me to extract all possible fun out of life. There are so many funny things around us, I don't want to miss any of them. AMEN"

"I thank you again for this great honor. I may forget everything else that has happened to me during the past 70 years but I shall never forget this day!"

Maxwell Sackheim

Address Given To The Largo Kiwanis Club
By Guest Speaker Maxwell Sackheim

December 6, 1976

"I was born in Russia in 1890. My IBM computer says I am 86 years old; but you can't always believe those modern gadgets. According to the insurance companies I've been dead for at least 15 years, but they must have punched the wrong hole in my statistic card. Actually I induced my parents to sail to these shores when I was only six months old, so you see I've been here longer than most of you, even though I still retain my Russian accent. I must apologize for referring to my notes instead of speaking from memory. Frankly I feel like Somerset Maughan must have felt when asked to speak on the occasion of his 80th birthday. At a gala dinner in his honor he said, three things seemed to have bothered him in recent years - one, he was beginning to lose his memory; then he added, he forgot what the other two were. That's why at my age I prefer to be a reader rather than an orator. So, with your kind indulgence I will try to give you at least 60 years of advertising experience in less than 30 minutes. This will be at a rate of more than two years per minute, so fasten your seat belts and hold on to your hats!"

A formula that has stood the test of at least 65 years within my observation.

"At the age of 15 I finished my formal education and got my first job as errand boy at $3 per week. I fell in love with advertising because it seemed to involve no physical or mental effort and the writers in the office looked prosperous. One day one of them gave me a copy of a book entitled, THE PSYCHOLOGY OF ADVERTISING, by Professor Walter Dill Scott of Northwestern

University. Much of what Professor Scott said has since become obsolete, what with the advent of radio, television, good roads, supermarkets, prize contests, shopping centers, trading stamps and other modern marketing methods. But he did advance a formula for successful advertising of all kinds and in all media - a formula that has stood the test of at least 65 years within my observation. To be successful, Professor Scott said advertising must ATTRACT, INTEREST, CONVINCE AND INDUCE ACTION."

"As part payment to the advertising business, I decided to write a book about my advertising experiences. Naturally I kept putting it off until one night before dropping off to sleep I picked up my bedside copy of the Holy Bible and turned to its pages at random. My eyes alighted on this sentence; *'Judas went out and hanged himself.'* I didn't think that was very inspiring so I closed the book and opened it again only to read, *'go thou and do likewise.'* Well, that disturbed me even more so I tried again and came across this sentence, *'what thou doest, do quickly.'* Then instead of hanging myself 'quickly,' I chanced to turn to Numbers, chapter 24, verse 14, where I found a reference to advertising. There Balaam, the prophet is recorded as having said to Balak, King of Moab, 'I will advertise thee what this people shall do to my people in the latter days.' I am not capable of translating that into modern language but according to my references, Balaam was resisted by the ass he rode for which the ass was smitten three times while the Angel of Jehovah stood in the way of its progress."

"Professor Scott's first lesson in advertising also had to do with a stubborn mule, the owner of which wanted to train it. He took a hefty length of a 2x4, and like Balaam smote the mule three times. When asked why he did it he said, 'before I can get this critter to listen to me, I have to attract his attention, don't I?'"

It may not result in the sale because it is necessary to attract favorable attention.

"Before you can deliver your message you must first get your prospect's attention! Now there are many ways to do this: You can cry *fire*, or *help*, or yell *free*, or you can stand on your head in front of your place of business, or you can use a 2x4 on various parts of your prospect's anatomy. I do not recommend the latter device for it may not result in the sale because it is necessary to attract FAVORABLE attention."

What has made this the most successful sales item in the history of civilization?

"Strange as it may seem, this little incident inspired me to delve further and further into the Old and New Testaments for clues as to why and what has made the Book of Books the most successful sales item in the history of civilization! I kept reading the Bible closely and when an opportunity came for me to visit the Holy Land I thought it would be a wonderful prelude to the months of work that lay ahead of me in the writing of my book. While sightseeing there I kept wondering what advertising lessons we could learn from the Holy Bible. Naturally we were tremendously and reverently impressed by everything we saw. Instead of a hazy dream the Bible became alive. We marched up the hills to Zion, climbed the slopes to Jerusalem, walked the narrow streets of Nazareth and sailed across the sea of Galilee. We saw pillars and monuments and towers centuries old everywhere and places where Jesus performed miracles. These were real and have been authenticated by numerous physical evidences of the past, many with hieroglyphic and cuneiform writings which have enabled scholars to confirm the thousands of years of Biblical lore. I must confess before my visit to the Holy Land I knew little more about the area than a child who, when asked where the Red Sea was, replied, 'Its on the third line on my report card.'"

"If it seems blasphemous or sacrilegious to associate the Bible with advertising, let me remind you that the Book of Books has been the source of advice on almost every imaginable subject so why not on advertising? The Bible belongs to us all. Among the numerous laws that protect and control us concerning adultery, arson, assault and judaical authority all the way down to wages, weights, measures, wills and the oath of witnesses, many have their root in Biblical Law. Our speech is dotted with words and phrases often attributed to Shakespeare and others; for example, 'The skin of my teeth', 'sour grapes', 'cast your bread upon the waters', 'no man can serve two masters', sufficient unto the day is the evil thereof', 'a house divided against itself cannot stand', and hundreds of other every day conversational gems come from the Bible. Our art and

115

literature has thrived for centuries on the wealth of themes so richly treated in the Bible. The number of paintings, poems, dramas, stories and novels inspired by narratives in the Bible is overwhelming. After 2000 years the Bible has been translated into more than 1100 languages and dialects and gives no sign of having exhausted its triumphant progress."

Compare this record with the history of any other product you can think of.

"Long before printing was invented. Ages before newspapers or magazines were available for advertising. Without the aid of radio, television, billboards or skywriting the Bible became the world's best seller and still is, despite the competition for our time from all sides. The Bible has ATTRACTED more people, INTERESTED more people, CONVINCED more people, and INDUCED more people to do something about it than any other force in the history of mankind. Compare this record with the history of any other product you can think of."

"So actually, the first advertising lesson to be gleaned from the history, influence and vitality of the Bible is that it behooves us to be sure we're offering something people will buy and be satisfied with so they will continue to buy. Unless your product or service, or idea, has a good reason for existence, unless it is a better value, newer, bigger, more convenient, more comfortable, more satisfying or more something or other, you may as well shut up shop before you begin."

You must keep your prospects interested and that's extremely difficult.

"After making certain your product is right and your method of attracting the public's attention is effective, you must keep your prospects interested and that's extremely difficult. Everyone of us is equipped with an automatic gadget similar to the one used on some radio and television sets. You press a button and silence the commercial. Our personal gadget is indifference and inertia. We glance at headlines and pictures with one eye, we listen with half an ear, we meet people and forget their names at once - if we get them at all. We read books and see plays and we're bored unless there is something very special about them. We go through life with our minds only half turned on. Our attitude generally about nearly everything is 'so what' and that hurdle must be taken at every step in the process of getting people to pay attention to what you are saying! To induce your prospects to drop everything else in order to listen to, or read your story, you must SHOCK, STARTLE, PROMISE them an adequate reward."

"You must shake people out of their complacency. We hate to change our minds, our habits, our routines. It takes tons of persuasion to get us to do or think what we WANT to do or think, to say nothing of the effort involved in shifting our mental gears to accommodate YOU. The best way to interest people is to direct your appeal to your prospect's interest NOT yours."

These are quite a let down from what we find in the Bible.

"Modern advertising writers should blush for shame when they compare their appeals with the lifelines in the Bible. In one issue of a prominent and expensive magazine some advertisers expected you and me, and millions of others, to be interested in such drivel as, and I quote, 'Its so lovely', 'The best riding car of them all', 'Arise to fluffier flapjacks', 'Is tomato juice most of the struggle', The best candy you ever tasted', 'Morning is sure to come', 'The choice of those who know', 'You're welcome - You're welcome - You're welcome.' These are quite a let down from what we find in the Bible."

"'Behold, how good and how pleasant it is for brethren to dwell together in unity', 'Even a fool when he holdeth his peace is counted wise', 'Train up a child in the way he should go, and when he is old he will not depart from it', 'They shall beat their swords into plowshares and their spears into pruning hooks', 'Nations shall not lift up sword against nation, neither shall they learn war anymore'."

"As to the length of sales appeal, listen to this: The longest verse in the Old Testament consists of 90 words. The longest verse in the New Testament embraces 68 words. The shortest verse in the Bible consists of just two words of nine letters - 'Jesus wept'."

"Advertising to be profitable must not only attract and interest. It must convince. Conviction depends upon believability. No matter what you say if it isn't believed, you've lost your sale.

Believability is born of sincerity. Don't underestimate the intelligence of the average person. Even if you succeed in selling by overselling, you may be losing a customer, and success or failure of your business depends upon the number of customers you make not upon the number of initial sales. Even an uneducated person's understanding vocabulary is much greater than his speaking vocabulary. As the Bible says, 'Great is Truth' and 'Mighty above all things', 'And the Truth shall make you free.' And the truth will make your advertising believed. The Bible has lived because it has been believed and it will continue to live because it cannot be denied."

These things cost nothing but they are the ingredients of successful advertising.

"From the cradle to the grave, in one way or another our advertising proclaims our virtues, displays our faults, builds or destroys good will. We profit or lose by the kind of advertising we do. One of the Bible Proverbs says: 'A merry heart maketh a cheerful countenance', also 'The heart of a man changes his countenance for good or evil.' And a smile today may be your best ad. Every time you speak you advertise yourself for better or worse. By the way, how good a listener are you? A good salesman sells by listening as well as by talking. Do you make your prospects feel comfortable by your attitude, speech and actions? Do you use a soft voice even when necessary to be tough? As the Bible says, 'A soft voice turneth away wrath.' Nearly everything about you advertises you - the lettering on your door, the letters you write and the ones you don't write, the appearance of your office, the way your telephone is answered, the way you remember or forget names and faces. Do you take yourself too seriously? Or, do you have a sense of humor? Do you have a hidden contempt for other people and their complex? Do you give orders and instructions so they are clearly understood or are people in a fog after you tell them what you want? There are countless other ways to advertise successfully. You know them as well as, or better than, any advertising man. Courtesy is advertising. Promptness is advertising. Tolerance is advertising. You can advertise favorably even when you must say no if you say it graciously. These things cost nothing but they are the ingredients of successful, personal advertising. These basic rules of conduct are all in the Bible.

The Letters you write and the ones you don't write.

Finally, and most important, your advertising must make a worthwhile promise to your prospects. You must emphasize what you do for your customer, not what they can do for you. As my protege, and old friend, Victor Schwab put it:"

As Victor Schwab put it:

I see you've spent quite a big wad of dough to tell me the things you think I should know. How your plant is so big, so fine and so strong and your founders had whiskers so handsomely long.

So he started the business in old '92. How tremendously interesting that is - to you. He built up the thing with the blood of his life! (I'll run home like mad, tell that to my wife!)

Your machinery's modern and oh so complete. Your "Rep" is so flawless; your workers so neat. Your motto is "Quality".... capital "Q", no wonder I'm tired of your "your" and "you".

So tell me quick and tell me true (or else my love to hell with you). Less ... "How this product came to be" more ... "What the damn thing does for me!"

Will it save me money or time or work, or hike up my pay with a welcome jerk? What drudgery, worry, or loss will it cut? Can it yank me out of a personal rut?

Perhaps it can make my appearance so swell that my telephone calls will wear out the bell; and thus it might win me a lot of fine friends (And one never knows where such a thing ends!)

I wonder how much it could do for my health? Could it show me a way to acquire some wealth? Better things for myself, for the kids and the wife, or how to quit work somewhat early in life?

So tell me quick and tell me true (or else my love to hell with you), Less ... "How this product came to be" More ... "What the damn thing does for me!"

"Yes, it pays to advertise if you have a good product that benefits the purchaser and you are honest in promoting it. This is what creates repeat sales. When in doubt, take a look into your Bible!"

A Personal Letter From Max Sackheim

On the next page is a letter that Max wrote to Jerry Buchanan just prior to his visit to the Portland area. He and his lovely wife, Mary, visited with Jerry and his family for an entire afternoon.

This letter has been reproduced so you can see Max's personal letterhead. It certainly sums up his experience in the field of advertising.

MAXWELL SACKHEIM

Advertising Consultant

801 West Bay Drive - Suite 339 - Largo, Florida 33540   Phone (813) 585-

AUTHOR

My First 65 Years
In Advertising

Seven Deadly
Advertising
Mistakes

Seven Deadly
Direct Mail
Mistakes

How To
Advertise
Yourself

ORIGINATOR

Book-Of-The-Month
Club

Around the World
Shoppers Club

American Express
Credit Card

Arthur Murray
Dancing Schools

National Music
Lovers Record
Club

Etc., Etc., Etc.

EXPERIENCE

Sears, Roebuck & Co.

Literary Guild

Sherwin Cody
School of English

Columbia Record
Club

Davis Fish Co.

Dollar Book Club

Doubleday & Co.

Funk & Wagnalls
Encyclopedia

Jackson & Perkins
(Rose Growers)

Little Leather
Library

Salvation Army
(Fund Raising)

Saltwater Farms
(Live Lobster
Shippers)

And many other
Mail Order
and
Direct Response
Advertising
Campaigns

June 19, 1978

Mr. Jerry Buchanan
6816 Middle Way
Vancouver, Washington 98664

Dear Jerry:

Many thanks for yours of the 15th. I will most
assuredly phone you as soon as convenient after our
arrival in the west. We leave here on Wednesday and
may arrive in Portland even before this letter
reaches you! At least we may arrange for a "hello"
meeting almost any time between then and July 5 when
we are scheduled to return to Florida.

Am sure the earth will not stop revolving while I'm
on the west coast and I promise to take up only a
few minutes of your time while there. Visitors are
a nuisance -- there "ought to be a law........." but
I promise not to be in your way.

Sincerely,

Maxwell

Maxwell Sackheim

MS:z

Don't sell the product, sell the benefit it will create.

-- Maxwell B. Sackheim

An Excerpt From The Life of Maxwell Sackheim

Andi Emerson, President of the Emerson Marketing Agency, Inc. in New York City, and Max Sackheim, were very good friends. She supplied the following letter she received from Max about a humorous incident that happened to him. It demonstrates his sparkling wit even at age 86.

MAX'S LETTER TO ANDI:

"Dear Andi:

This is the funniest thing that ever happened to me. I read this ad in *Ad Age*, answered it, and did not hear anything further until two years later.

This contact resulted in my earning a fee of $500 for writing a letter. There was something "funny" about this deal but I made no protest -- just accepted the check and the honor they paid me by seeking so publicly for my "equal." I really began to appreciate myself after this ad: Thought you'd be interested.

Sincerely,

Max"

THE STORY:

The following is the ad Max came across while reading his issue of *Ad Age*:

"WANTED: THE MAXWELL SACKHEIM OF THE 70'S.

Our requirements are very simple. ALL we want is a modern-day Maxwell Sackheim. A creator of direct mail pieces, catalogues and display ads that SELL back-to-the-country, down-home, environmentally oriented magazines, books merchandise and food. If you can write REAL direct-response copy that SELLS, you want to join a dynamically expanding operation and you'd like to live in the beautiful mountains of western North Carolina ... send us samples of your best work and your salary requirements. We'll take it from there."

Box 0000 ADVERTISING AGE"
708 Third Avenue,
New York, New York 10017

MAX'S REPLY:

"Gentlemen:

I read with great interest your Help Wanted advertisement in the July 22 issue of *Advertising Age* and would like to be considered for the position.

I have known Maxwell Sackheim for many years, have followed his career from the time he obtained his first job in advertising and even before then while we were attending grade school in Chicago. I watched his progress at Ruthrauff & Ryan in New York, where he created the famous Sherwin Cody School of English ad, and later his association with Harry Scherman as Co-Founder of little Leather Library, Book-of-the-Month Club, National Music Lovers (the first record club, I believe), and later as President of Brown Fence & Wire Company of Cleveland, Ohio (where he spent a number of years), and then as the owner of the Maxwell Sackheim Advertising Agency in New York where he did the advertising for *Literary Guild*, American Express Credit Cards, Columbia Record Club, Doubleday & Co., Jackson & Perkins, Dollar Book Club, Saltwater Farms (live lobsters by mail) and many other direct response projects. Some of Mr. Sackheim's experience must have had its effect on me. It would have been impossible for me to have lived so close to Maxwell without having absorbed some of his "genius." While I am not seeking steady employment and while I am not as young or as active as I once was. I still would like to keep my mind young. I'm sure Mr. Sackheim would recommend me to you for an occasional assignment, to help solve a problem, establish a sales plan, prepare an ad or mailing, or merely to confer with you at your 'beautiful spot in the mountains of Western North Carolina.'

The reason I speak so confidently about Maxwell Sackheim's opinion of me is because I am

Sincerely yours,

Maxwell Sackheim

P.S. If you have not read my book entitled *"MY FIRST SIXTY YEARS IN ADVERTISING"* I will be glad to send you an autographed copy with my compliments in part payment for honoring me with your ad."

M.S.

*A*dvertising is nothing more than salesmanship in print. -- (or via any type of media - the editor.)

-- **John E. Kennedy**

Ads That Are Welcome

By Maxwell Sackheim
July 17, 1981

Advertising admired by the advertiser is too frequently ignored by consumers! The test of good copy is the result it accomplishes, and the only real experts are the public. The approval of customers can be measured by traceable sales or other evidences of interest such as requests for further information, telephone calls or sales through dealers or other distributors.

There are certain established directions for writing the kind of advertising that has proven in the past to be most effective in obtaining responses. The advertising writer of today need not start from "scratch" to find out what basic elements "attract, interest, convince and induce action". There are many precedents for writing attention-compelling headlines, for writing convincing copy, and for the use of "words that work" as the writer wants them to.

The difference will be in the number of prospects who read beyond the headlines.

There isn't much difference between good copywriters except their ability or skill in preparing headlines. Given the average piece of merchandise to describe or sell, two good copy men will do about the same kind of job. The difference will be in the number of prospects who read beyond the headlines. By switching their headlines (if there is a marked difference between them) you can completely reverse results.

My personal test of a headline is always whether or not the reader, in response, gets a "so what" reaction. If he does, you can almost gamble that it is not good. If, on the other hand, the reader is compelled to ask WHAT, WHO, WHERE, WHEN, WHY, or

HOW, it is likely to be effective in inducing the reader to read the rest of the ad.

In broader terms, the acid test is whether or not the headline induces reading of the ad. Cleverness alone may actually be harmful. The best headlines are usually those which incorporate strong, small words. The strongest word is still the word "FREE". From this there are many variations such as "without charge -- given -- yours -- accept -- take it -- for you, etc."

Next to the word "free" the best word is "NEW". Other tested words are "Stop -- At Last -- Don't -- Here -- Now -- Earn -- Crazy -- Easy -- Pain -- Ruin -- Pay -- Sweetheart -- Selfish -- Jealous -- Money -- Science -- First".

Generally speaking a question is better than a statement. And all headlines definitely should promise information.

Of course the thought in the headline is more important than any word but the right words make the thought penetrate.

The best headlines are usually those which incorporate strong, small words.

What is said about headline writing is equally true of letter writing. Your opening sentence may make or break your letter, no matter what is said afterwards.

Your opening sentence may make or break your letter, no matter what is said afterwards.

There are, of course, exceptions. Occasionally a powerful illustration will in itself be more effective than any headline that could be written. A striking layout may occasionally do the trick. But, if an ad lends itself to the use of a headline at all, the headline should never cause a "so what" reaction.

Advertising, even a package of gum to say nothing of more expensive and more complicated items, should complete its selling job by endeavoring in some way to maintain contact with the reader, provided the advertiser has more of a story to tell than can be told in the ad itself.

For example, food products lend themselves to an offer of recipe books to be sent free, or for a self-liquidating sum. Wearing apparel lends itself to an offer of style booklets. Household equipment presents endless possibilities for offering additional selling literature. Cosmetics lend themselves to offers of more beauty secrets, etc.

The best offer may be a free sample or a ten-cent sample, if conspicuously presented (to keep the curiosity hounds away). In some cases the offer can be to ship merchandise direct "if not obtainable through dealers". Or the merchandise may adapt itself to elaborate and valuable literature for which a charge can be made. But in practically every instance an offer of some kind should be considered if it will enable the advertiser to do a more thorough selling job at least on those who write.

Unless the story is complete, unless the ad tells all the advertiser has to say, it should offer additional information. Responses from readers can certainly do little if any harm. The cost of answering inquiries can be kept within bounds. And inquiries can be made to serve many useful purposes.

I have never been able to understand why so many advertisers are afraid to use long copy when there's so much evidence to prove its value; so much in fact that the only reason for using short copy is when there isn't much to say.

If you can tell your story in ten words, fine. But if you need a thousand words nothing less is fair to the space you pay for..

One good test of copy is whether or not it can be cut. If it can be cut, cut it. But when cutting is hard work, you are getting down to bedrock. Tell your story fully and completely. If you can tell it in ten words, fine. But if you need a thousand words nothing less is fair to the space you pay for.

Use your imagination! Put yourself in your prospective customer's place. If you are a typical prospect, be yourself -- and appeal to yourself! Good advertising is the product of a fertile imagination. Be daring and the world may beat a path to your door.

Maxwell Sackheim

Okay - you've just finished a swell piece of copy. Would you buy the product or service you've tried to sell? Remember: Other people aren't in love with your words.

-- Copy Capsules

Seven Deadly Advertising Mistakes

MISTAKE #1

Give the Reader a Reason for Not Reading:

"Just another ad" is just another advertising tragedy.

Advertising does not command attention merely *because* it is advertising. Unless readers are given a substantial *reason* for reading an advertisement, they will give it no more than a passing glance. "Just another ad" is just another advertising tragedy.

It is astonishing how many advertisements FAIL to give the reader a single *incentive* to read them. Still worse, many advertisements actually *kill* interest in themselves at the very first glance.

This may be due to the general appearance of the ad - too "regular," too dull, too blatant, too obviously a selfish attempt to *sell*.

It may be due to the *headline* or to the *illustration*.

Whatever it is that makes the reader turn away quickly, destroys the value of the advertisement!

Unless an ad promises something to make reading worthwhile it isn't good advertising.

The basis of practically all successful advertising is NEWS. It may be a BARGAIN - or HEALTH - or WEALTH - or LOVE - or ACCLAIM - or any other human emotion, ambition or desire. But unless an ad PROMISES something to make the reading worthwhile it isn't good advertising.

Yet many advertisements promise nothing!

Actually, many advertisements simply and quickly say: "I'm not important."

Does it promise anything as a reward for reading it?

Test the advertisements in any issue of any magazine or newspaper by this one standard: Does it *promise* anything as a reward for reading it? See how few are genuinely appealing. See how MANY commit the sin of actually telling you why you should NOT read them!

Beware of Deadly Advertising Mistake NO. 1. *Never give the reader a chance to say "NO" before you even get started!*

MISTAKE #2

Use Headlines That Whisper Sweet Nothings:

Many advertising *headlines* are *dead* lines.

They sleep peacefully, never stirring, never arousing the slightest interest.

Instead of creating an irresistible desire to find out more - they stop us from wanting to read further.

Instead of *demanding* a reading, these lazy, hazy headlines prevent reading. Instead of creating an irresistible desire to find out *more*, they act as *"stoppers"* - stopping us from *wanting* to read further.

The difference in headlines can easily make a two-to-one difference in readership - and in *results* - as has been proved again and again by advertising which could be *measured by actual responses.*

When twice as many people respond to one advertisement as to another, both being identical except for the headline, the *only* conclusion one can come to is that one headline is asleep and other awake - one headline shirks and the other works, one is a wet blanket, the other a spark!

The more people that read an ad, the more they, in the aggregate, will be convinced by it.

Since this is true of advertising which can be *measured* it is equally true of advertising which directs customers to stores; the more people that *read* an ad, the more they, in the aggregate, will be *convinced* by it.

People are busy. Their time for reading is limited. Their interests are extremely narrow. A headline that doesn't hit them between the eyes earns only a fleeting glance. Readers refuse to get excited about things which are *unimportant to them.*

The headline that isn't read doesn't give the ad itself a chance!

The reason so many headlines are dull, flat,, uninteresting, is that writers become "clever"; or they brag ; or they take too much for granted; or they think the public *owes* them a reading. In short, they *promise* nothing. And the headline that isn't read doesn't give the ad itself a chance!

In one issue of a national magazine, headlines similar to the following appeared; can *you* get excited over any of them? They represented several hundred thousand dollars invested in space! Granted, the illustrations are missing, but we'll talk about pictures later. Meanwhile, what do you get out of these *headlines?*

It's so lovely ...
Aha! A Frenchman who doesn't drink ...
The best riding car of them all!
The best candy you ever tasted
Going somewhere, mister?
Meet America's Snappiest New Car
Try us!
Easter means ---- Candies!
The choice of those who know
Mom said, Come and *stay* with us!
Reflect man, REFLECT!
New - and Styled for the future
My Big Day Has Come Again
Less Trouble - Greater Durability
Demand ------ Tires, because they Wear Longer
An Old Idea in New Clothes

This Wardrobe Magician is Helpful All Year Long
When you're at the wheel of a tough steer
Baby's Best Friend

Imagine "headlines" like these in *one* issue - competing with each other, competing with ads that carry *infinitely* better headlines, competing with the editorial content of the magazine.

How much attention could these headlines get? How much *news* do they contain? What do they promise?

The headline that whispers sweet nothings is Deadly Advertising Mistake No. 2.

MISTAKE #3

Use Pictures That Do Not Talk:

Twisting the old Chinese adage, "10 words are worth a thousand pictures - if they're the right words and the wrong pictures."

If a picture doesn't tell a story or complete a story, it isn't the right picture.

Unless an illustration is self-explanatory, or gives meaning to the words, it shouldn't be used. If a picture doesn't tell a story by itself, or doesn't complete the story by the headline, it isn't the right picture.

To use illustrations merely because an ad "ought to have a picture in it" is one of the greatest of all advertising fallacies.

Illustrations are *most quickly* read. Therefore they must be *right* - and therefore, it is better to use *no* picture than to use the wrong one.

It may focus attention upon itself at the expense of the product advertised.

If a photograph or drawing *doesn't* tell a story it may make the entire ad seem unimportant.

In plain words an "addy" illustration frequently destroys the desire to *read.* It labels an ad "just another ad." It may be so attractive that it focuses attention upon itself at the expense of the product advertised.

If an illustration meets the requirements of *copy* it's good. Ask yourself, "is it news?" Does it convey a *promise?* Does it enlighten or entertain? Is it closely related to the theme of the ad or is it "lugged in"? Is it being used just because it is "attractive," or "cute" or to "arouse curiosity?"

A picture must do a *job* to earn its space value! There must be a valid *reason* for its use. If an ad is "dry and uninteresting" without a picture there may be something wrong with the headline or the theme. A picture should be a *plus*, not a crutch!

Whenever intelligent advertisers face a crisis they really try to do a selling job.

Whenever intelligent advertisers face a *crisis* they really try to do a selling job. Fancy pictures are discarded. "Beautiful layouts" are thrown out. They *fight* to sell. Well, isn't the search for *more* sales critical to most companies? Why not treat *sales* as a crisis?

I have no quarrel with art directors but they shouldn't be permitted to dominate advertising.

Pictures - and copy - *must* fit. If they are *misfits* they are costly and ineffective. Pictures must *talk.*

In actual tests we have proved that even *color* advertising can be less effective than black and white, perhaps because color frequently emphasizes the "addiness" of an ad!

Deadly Advertising Mistake No. 3 is to permit a *silent picture* or an *inappropriate layout* to be used. Tell your story first, then use a picture that fits - or the opposite - or none.

MISTAKE #4

The Curse of Cleverness:

It is a rare product that can win customers through these devices.

Clever plays on words and attempts to be funny in advertising usually fall flat. There is a place for cleverness and humor, but it is a rare product that can win customers through these devices. The more clever and the more humorous, the more they may detract from the selling effect!

For example, someone once started a vogue of "comparisons." Now, when all else fails, some advertising campaigns resort to the "comparison" idea.

Let's see how we can compare our product with something accepted as the epitome of "great beauty."

Or, perhaps "great beauty" is the theme. Well, let's see how we can compare our product with something accepted as the epitome of "great beauty." Dogs! That's it! Let's show gorgeous drawings or photographs of prize-winning dogs and compare our product with them!

Often the comparison is unfavorable to the product because it is so obviously a glorified form of bragging.

Another form of "copy-cleverness" is the "Smart Alec" type. Sometimes this is combined with an illustration. In a recent issue of one magazine I found several examples of "cleverness" similar to the following:

> You talking to me?
> A Leaf for the Chief
> Powder Room Chit Chat
> Here's the chap who took the stroll
> A Gleaming Sample
> Speaking of Revolutions
> A Woman's Face Begins at Home
> Boy are We Men Lucky
> Really squeally yummy
> My how bright! What a sight!

Here's the Mrs. Bringing Home the Bakin
Everyone wants a share
Thrift Pays for Luxuries
Food for Thought
What Makes a Man Tops?
Pecos Sam isn't bulldoggin' today

"Cute" ads may attract attention, but if too far removed from the selling job they may cease to become salesmen.

"Cute" ads may attract attention, but if too far removed from the main selling job they cease to become salesmen.

"Copy-cleverness," to paraphrase an old slogan, "may be remembered long after the product is forgotten." Beware of Deadly Advertising Mistake No. 4 - The Curse of Cleverness.

MISTAKE #5

Go All Around Robin's Barn

When a thought must reach the brain through a series of intricate mental switches, gears, cams, springs and motors, it's a poor conductor of an idea.

Too much advertising is designed to sneak up on an unsuspecting reader!

Too much advertising is designed to *sneak* up on an unsuspecting reader! For example, an ad asks "what do these motions mean?" It illustrates and explains that the motions referred to mean "speed it up" in a moving picture studio.

The clash of gears, the throwing of switches, and the ponderous movement of the mind is expected to take place when the advertiser reveals at last that he is selling automobile polish.

Here is another: Picture of a cow jumping over the moon headlined "Above all-it's Malted Oats for quality." And another, "Jonesy wants to get into the act." And still another: "Savings Pay the Bill." And further: "The Romans Knew," "Dear Diary Don't Tell on Me," "Giddap Horsie. Let's Go Places," "No Bigger Than a Minute".

It should not make it necessary for the reader to turn mental handsprings to find out what is being advertised.

An ad should certainly try to sell the merchandise advertised. It can do this best by avoiding the need for charts or diagrams to clarify a tricky approach. It should not make it necessary for the reader to turn mental handsprings to find out what is being advertised.

This does not mean that if you have shirts to sell you must instantly describe the material and display the price. You may decide that more men want glamour than shirts. The "sizzle," as Wheeler say's, may be your merchandise. But whatever it is, don't try to sell it by showing a cow jumping over the moon - unless you are selling a cow that *can* jump over the moon!

The roundabout approach is usually an advertising mistake. It seldom gets the reader on track to a sale!

MISTAKE #6

Leave 'em Dangling:

Why do so many ads leave the reader dangling in midair? If they read an ad and are *convinced* by it, why risk a forgetting-time instead of providing a *getting* time.

What possible objection can there be to making an offer in every ad?

What possible objection can there be to making an offer in every ad? Offer a booklet, or circular, or a sample, or a *sale* if possible. Give the reader a chance to do something immediately to "clinch" the "sale" your ad made.

If your merchandise does not have universal distribution you may be justified in offering it for *sale* direct to the consumer "if not available at your dealer's."

Instead of giving the reader the "go-by" give them the GO-BUY!

Advertising can lose much of its value because of inertia. People intend to do certain things, intend to buy certain products, but forget, neglect to, or change their minds between the time they were "sold" and the time they intended to buy! Advertising can urge the public to go to their drug, department, hardware, or other store, but it can also make it possible for them to order direct, if they prefer to do so. If desired, sales can then be turned over to the nearest dealer. Instead of giving the reader the "go-by" give them the GO-BUY!

Out of 131 advertisements in an issue of a large national publication, eighty-eight contained no offer to the reader.

Advertising should complete the selling job by endeavoring in some way to maintain contact with the reader.

For example, food products lend themselves to an offer of recipe books, to be sent free, or for a self-liquidating sum. Wearing apparel lends itself to an offer of style booklets. Household equipment presents endless possibilities for offering additional selling literature. Cosmetics lend themselves to offers of more "beauty secrets," etc.

But in practically every instance an offer of some kind should be considered, if it will enable the advertiser to do a more thorough selling job.

The best offer may be a free sample, a ten-cent sample, or a self-liquidating "box top" offer. Or the merchandise may be such as to justify a charge. But in practically every instance an offer of some kind should be considered, if it will enable the advertiser to do a more thorough selling job.

If the offer is only of a folder containing larger illustrations than are shown in an advertisement, it may be advantageous to invite the reader to write. The very act of writing helps fasten a name in the prospect's memory.

Even if only to analyze the relative readership of various ads and the relative pulling power of publications, or different positions, reader response is worth while. No one can convince me that an ad which induces a thousand people to "write for a special recipe book" hasn't been more widely read than an ad which brings in only a hundred such requests under approximately the same conditions.

Invite the reader to write for "more information," or "name of dealer near you," or for "illustrated brochure," or for "prices," or for a sample," or for the merchandise itself at a quoted price. Invite them to clip or tear out a coupon bearing the name of your product, as a "reminder" to go to their dealer. That's what we mean by direct response. It costs you nothing extra.

Never leave the reader dangling! They may fall in a competitor's lap!

MISTAKE #7

Use "Yackety-Yack" Copy:

You've met the garrulous individual whose words slipped off your mind like water off a duck's back. Courtesy provided him an audience - so he kept talking, not realizing that you weren't listening.

But if he writes that way- you can get away quickly!

You may tolerate the gabby guy who pounds your ear with verbal "tripe." But if he *writes* that way - you can get away quickly! You don't have to "take it." Nor does anyone else.

Many advertisers, realizing the futility of empty claims, or meaningless verbiage, cut their copy to a few words. Their ads became "reminders-of-the-name." They use *billboards* in magazines. Though I disagree with this technique, it is better than filling an ad with "drivel."

We do not belong to the "write as you talk" school - but neither do we belong to the "average age of intelligence" school. We live in a literate country and the most stupid mistake a writer can make is to underestimate the discrimination of the public.

It takes more than a glib tongue, and a free flowing pen, to make people swallow a string of "just words."

Advertising must be believable. It takes more than a glib tongue, and a free-flowing pen, to make people swallow self-praise or a string of "just words." Stop patting yourself on the back. Stop talking for the sake of hearing your own voice. If you have something to say, SAY it, but don't insult the reader's intelligence by trying to double-talk them into thinking your product is what they should buy.

For example, here are a few paragraphs, similar to many which have appeared in advertisements. While it is true that some of their force and meaning may be lost when separated from the entire advertisements in which they appeared, anyone will admit that these paragraphs are empty.

"Crafted with the knowing sureness of artistic insight .... bubbling with a whirlpool of iridescent beauty ... rich, luxurious wools from every corner of the globe, specially treated to retain their inherent 'bounce'. So luxurious in look and feel they become the embodiment of dignity ... adding their own virtues to all who possess them."

"As restless as a panther ... rippling in the glowing approbation of the sun, meteor-like the - comes whirling into your life."

"What is the one gift your sweetie dreams about, twenty four hours a day? How can you be as tactful as a diplomat, as foresighted as a fortune teller, as timely as the first day of Spring?"

When words clutter up whatever impression the rest of the ad may have created, *cut them out!*

The great challenge to copywriters is to find something to say that will be worth the reader's while.

The great challenge to copywriters is to find something to say that will be worth the reader's while. Failing this, why resort to "filler" copy? It may be lots better to use a few words than "Yackety-Yack" copy.

Ask Yourself These Questions About Your Advertising

1) Does it give the reader a reason for not reading?
2) Am I using headlines that whisper sweet nothings?
3) Am I using pictures that do not talk?
4) Is my advertising cursed with cleverness?
5) Does my approach go, all around Robin's barn?
6) Do my advertisements leave 'em dangling?
7) Do my advertisements contain "Yackety-Yack" copy?

Why should anyone read your advertising? Is it NEWS? Does it PROMISE anything of importance to the reader? Or is it just another ad"?

Why should anyone believe your advertising? Are you really convincing - or just "talky"?

Why should anyone do anything about your advertising? Do you give 'em a chance or do you leave 'em high and dry?

In summary:

Paint a word picture of the prospect's dilemma and then describe how your product will solve it IN THE SIMPLEST, MOST DIRECT WORDS POSSIBLE!!! Don't try to be poetic. Be a realist and you'll sell a lot more product.

Ideas for Writing Great Ads

This period was considered by many as the Golden Age of advertising.

This section contains many special ads written between 1915 and 1930. This period was considered by many as the Golden Age of advertising. Cost of advertising space was relatively low - therefore it was possible to use full pages of long, strong selling copy.

These ads were all written by either Maxwell Sackheim, Harry Scherman, or the other copywriters they employed at The Sackheim & Scherman Advertising Agency.

The reason for this section isn't just to look at some great old ads. Much more important is the education contained in each and every one. As you go through each ad, carefully look at each important component and its purpose.

As G. Lynn Sumner said in his book <u>How I Learned the Secrets of Success in Advertising</u> (Prentice-Hall 1952):

> New formulas are being created everyday, and the importance of continuously seeking for fresh, new formulas cannot be too strongly emphasized. But it is also true that successful advertising and selling are a sum-total of experience in all advertising and selling, and he who fails to study the successful methods of the past is risking all on hazardous chance. Remember: Styles change, times change, customs change, and tastes change - **but human nature, NEVER.**

Your advertising is bound to improve!

Study this section in detail and your advertising is bound to improve!

Ad #1: Sherwin Cody School of English

This is a smaller version of that famous full page ad Max Sackheim wrote in 1918 while employed at the Ruthrauff & Ryan Advertising Agency. The full page version is in book one. Let's look at the reason why this was such a famous ad that ran for over forty years.

The Headline: Do You Make These Mistakes in English?

1) It selects the proper audience with the words "Mistakes in ENGLISH". Targeted to anyone wanting to know if they make these particular mistakes in English.

2) It talks directly to you!

3) It offers information of value - a free lesson in English. It does this by using the word "these". The word "these" also arouses your curiosity as to what mistakes are contained below.

If you would like to see how one word can make or break an ad, take out the word "these". The ad now becomes "Do You Make Mistakes in English?" It takes on an entirely different appeal. Now it just sounds like an English lecture is about to follow.

Body of the ad:
The sub-headline tells you the benefit of having good English and how you can improve it at once. Then the first paragraph immediately starts to give you a lesson in English. Now you're to the point of wanting to read the rest of the ad. The free book and 15-minute test are just the right enticements to get you to send for step two of this two-step process. The free book and 15-minute test will further convince you that you need lessons in English.

The real reason this ad was such a success is because Max Sackheim transformed himself into the prospect. He was able to do this because he was already trying to improve his own English, so he wrote the ad to himself.

The amount of inquiries from this ad and the larger version is in the many millions (exact amount unknown).

Compare this smaller version to the larger one (see book one, page 32). Notice what has been removed without compromising the effectiveness of the ad.

Do You Make these Mistakes in ENGLISH?

Does your English reveal your lack of education or does it prove that you are a person of culture and refinement? English is the one weapon you must use every day. This tells how you can improve it almost at once.

MANY persons say, "Did you hear from him today." They should say, "Have you heard from him today?" Some persons spell calendar "calender" or "calander." Still others say, "between you and I" instead of "between you and me." It is astonishing how many persons use "who" for "whom" and mispronounce the simplest words. Few persons know whether to spell certain words with one or two "c's" or "m's" or "r's," or with "ie" or "ei," and when to use commas in order to make their meaning absolutely clear. And most persons use only common words—colorless, flat, ordinary. Their speech and their letters are lifeless, monotonous, humdrum. Every time they talk or write they show themselves lacking in the essential points of English.

SHERWIN CODY

WONDERFUL NEW INVENTION

For many years Mr. Cody studied the problem of creating instinctive habits of using good English. After countless experiments he finally invented a simple method by which you can acquire a better command of the English language in only 15 minutes a day. Now you can stop making the mistakes in English which have been hurting you. Mr. Cody's students have secured more improvement in five weeks than had previously been obtained by other pupils in two years!

LEARN BY HABIT—NOT BY RULES

Under old methods rules are memorized, but correct habits are not formed. Finally, the rules themselves are forgotten. The new Sherwin Cody method provides for the formation of correct habits by constantly calling attention only to the mistakes you make.

One of the wonderful things about Mr. Cody's course is the speed with which these habit-forming practice drills can be carried out. You can write the answers to fifty questions in 15 minutes and correct your work in five minutes more. The drudgery and work of copying have been ended by Mr. Cody. You concentrate always on your mistakes until it becomes "second nature" to speak and write correctly.

FREE BOOK ON ENGLISH AND 15-MINUTE TEST

A command of polished and effective English denotes education and culture. It wins friends and makes a favorable impression upon those with whom you come in contact. And now, in only 15 minutes a day—in your own home—you can actually check up and see yourself improve by using the 100% self-correcting method.

Mr. Cody has prepared a simple 15-minute test which you can take in your own home. The correct answers are given so you can tell at once just where you stand. If you are efficient in English it will give you greater confidence; if you are deficient you surely want to know it. Write to-day for this test—it is free. We will also gladly mail you our new free book, "How to Speak and Write Masterly English." Merely mail the coupon or a postal card.

SHERWIN CODY SCHOOL OF ENGLISH

383 Searle Building   Rochester, New York

- - - - - - - - - - - - - - - -

SHERWIN CODY SCHOOL OF ENGLISH
383 Searle Building, Rochester, N. Y.

Please send me your Free Book, "How to Speak and Write Masterly English," and also the 15-minute test.

Name ....

Address ....

City .... State..........

Ad #2: Sherwin Cody School of English

This ad ran in *The New Success* magazine April 1921. Sherwin Cody's advertising was under the control of The Sackheim & Scherman Advertising Agency.

With the exception of the headline, this ad is very similar to ad #1.

Headline: What Does Your English Tell About You?

1) The audience for this ad is selected by the words "Your English". Anyone interested in their own English is the target.

2) It again talks directly to you.

3) It arouses curiosity with "Tell About You"?. What Does Your English Tell About You? That question suggests that by reading further you may discover something about yourself that only your English can reveal.

The headline doesn't offer a free lesson in English even though the reader will still get one if they read the first paragraph.

Notice how the sub-headlines tell a complete story. It's a fact that some people buy without reading the entire ad. If your sub-headlines tell a story like this, you'll make sales and inquiries to the people who only skim through ads.

This ad was tested against "Do You Make these Mistakes in English?" The exact results are unknown. However, it did fall far short in gaining inquiries even though the only significant difference between these two ads is the headlines. Proving once again how changing only the headline of an ad can create two very different results.

It may be that the major difference between the two ads was that "these mistakes" offered something FREE -- if only a small self-test lesson, whereas Ad #2 did not and only appealed to snobbery.

What Does Your English Tell About You?

Does your English reveal your lack of education or does it prove that you are a man or woman of culture and refinement? Are you handicapped in your speech and writing or does your command of English rise to meet every occasion and every situation? English is the one weapon you must use every day. Here is how you can improve it almost at once.

MANY people say, "Did you hear from him to-day?" They *should* say, "Have you heard from him today?" Some say, "I didn't get your answer yet," instead of, "I haven't got your answer yet." Some people spell calendar *"calender"* or *"calander."* Still others say "between you and I," instead of "between you and me." It is astonishing how many people use "who" for "whom" and mispronounce the simplest words. Few people know whether to spell certain words with one or two "c's" or "m's" or "r's" or with "ie" or "ei," and when to use commas in order to make their meaning absolutely clear. And very few people use any but the most common words—colorless, flat, ordinary. Their speech and their letters are lifeless, monotonous, humdrum. Every time they talk or write they show themselves lacking in the essential points of English.

Every time you talk, every time you write, you show what you are. When you use the wrong word, when you mispronounce a word, when you punctuate incorrectly, when you use flat, ordinary words, you handicap yourself enormously. An unusual command of English enables you to present your ideas clearly, forcibly, convincingly. If your English is incorrect it hurts you more than you will ever know, for people are too polite to tell you about your mistakes.

Stop Making Mistakes

For the past five years Mr. Cody has been working almost day and night on the study of the problem, "How to make correct habits in speaking and writing stick in your mind." He appealed to school superintendents, and 150 of them placed classes at his disposal for experiment. He appealed to great corporations, and they let their employees be tested so Mr. Cody would know how accurate they really were. He was amazed to discover that the average person in school or in business is only 61% efficient in the vital points of English grammar. After countless experiments Mr. Cody finally invented a simple method by which you can acquire a better command of the English language in only 15 minutes a day. Now you can stop making the mistakes in English which have been hurting you. Mr. Cody's students have secured more improvement in five weeks than had previously been obtained by other pupils in two years!

Learn By Habit—Not By Rules

Mr. Cody has applied scientific principles to teaching the correct use of English. He made tens of thousands of tests of his various devices before inventing his present method. In all his tests he found that the trouble with old methods is that they do not stick in the mind. Rules are memorized, but correct habits are not formed. Finally the rules themselves are forgotten. The new Sherwin Cody method provides for the formation of correct habits by constantly calling attention only to the mistakes you make.

SHERWIN CODY

Only 15 Minutes a Day

One of the wonderful things about Mr. Cody's course is the speed with which these habit-forming practice drills can be carried out. You can write the answer to fifty questions in 15 minutes and correct your work in 5 minutes more. The drudgery and work of copying have been ended by Mr. Cody. Moreover, you do not have to go through page after page of material with which you are familiar. You concentrate always **on your mistakes** until it becomes "second nature" to speak and write correctly.

Write for Free Book

A booklet explaining Mr. Cody's remarkable Course is ready. If you are ever embarrassed by mistakes in grammar, spelling, pronunciation or punctuation, if you cannot instantly command the exact words with which to express your ideas, this book will prove a revelation to you.

A polished and effective command of the English language not only gives you the stamp of education, but it wins friends and impresses favorably those with whom you come in contact. Many men and women spend years in high school and years in college largely to get this key to social and business success. And now a really efficient system of acquiring an unusual command of English is offered to you. Spare time study—15 minutes a day—in your own home will give you power of language that will be worth more than you can realize.

Write for this new free book, "How to Speak and Write Masterly English." Merely mail the coupon or a letter or even a postal card. You can never reach your greatest possibilities until you use correct English. Write today for the free booklet that tells about Mr. Cody's simple invention.

SHERWIN CODY SCHOOL OF ENGLISH
104-A Searle Building, Rochester, N. Y.

- - - - - - - - - - - - - - - - - - -

SHERWIN CODY SCHOOL OF ENGLISH
104-A Searle Building,   Rochester, New York

Please send me your Free Book "How to Speak and Write Masterly English."

Name . . . .

Address . . . .

. . . .

Ad #3: Frank E. Davis, The Gloucester Fisherman

The Sackheim & Scherman Advertising Agency took over the advertising for Frank E. Davis in 1923. Frank Davis' business began to boom soon after. This ad was personally written by Maxwell Sackheim.

Headline: The Tastiest Ocean Treat from Gloucester *Plump, tender, juicy* **CHICKEN SALT MACKEREL FILLETS**

The reason this campaign was such a success is because the character of Frank E. Davis, a real Gloucester fisherman, was made very real to the readers. He spoke in the true language of a sea-faring man. His claims and his offers inspired confidence. And he guaranteed satisfaction.

Selling seafood through the mail is common today, but it wasn't in 1923. This ad helped sell millions of dollars worth of mackerel.

Every effective direct response ad takes advantage of as many of the five physical senses as possible. This one uses **taste** first -- Chicken-salted, broiled in its own juices -- then **aroma** - "smell of the fish fillets broiling in the pan", then **sight** "tender, full-bodied, to a tempting golden brown, late-caught" and using adjectives that actually make the reader's mouth water through hypnotic suggestion. The other perks and illustrations nail down the offer so it would be almost impossible to refuse to order.

The Tastiest Ocean Treat from Gloucester
plump, tender, juicy
CHICKEN SALT
MACKEREL
FILLETS

Sent on approval

I guarantee them to please you!

Just what you want for a hearty breakfast!

TASTE THEM AT MY EXPENSE

You'll never know how delicious fish can be until you serve some of my mackerel fillets, prepared the Down East way. It will be the rarest treat you've known in months. Take one of my new, small, meaty, late-caught mackerel fillets. Freshen it. Broil it in its own juices to a tempting brown, until the rich, tender meat falls apart at the touch of your fork. Serve piping hot. Your mouth will water at its appetizing aroma. You'll smack your lips over its wonderful flavor.

What Makes My Mackerel Fillets So Good?

But you must get the right kind of mackerel fillets —the pick of the new late catch is what you want— to get this real food joy. That's the secret of the tempting goodness of my mackerel fillets. I send you the choicest fillets that are carefully sliced from the fat, tender sides of the new late-caught mackerel. Practically boneless, no waste parts whatever, these mackerel fillets are so tender and full bodied that they just flake into juicy mouthfuls.

Send No Money Now—
unless you wish to

Just send the coupon below or write me a letter, and I'll ship you a pail of 18 small, tenderloin mackerel fillets—each fillet suitable for an individual serving. My fillets come to you all cleaned — no heads—no tails—no large body bones—no waste whatever —just meaty fillets packed in new brine in a wax-lined wooden pail. Taste one—broiled the Down East way. If not satisfied it's the finest mackerel you ever tasted, return the balance at my expense. Otherwise, send me only $2 within 10 days. 200,000 families get their seafood from me this "prove-it-yourself" way. I've been doing business this way

> **18**
> *Small, Tender*
> **Mackerel Fillets Only**
> **$2**⁰⁰
> Delivered FREE! Anywhere In the U. S.

for 49 years and I must say that this is the lowest price for this size pail of mackerel fillets I've ever offered. Send your coupon today for this real Gloucester treat.

Frank E. Davis, The Gloucester Fisherman
134 Central Wharf, Gloucester, Mass.

Ad #4: Arthur Murray Dance Studios

The Sackheim & Scherman Advertising Agency started selling Arthur Murray's dance lessons by mail. Arthur Murray became a huge success.

This ad ran in the December 1922 issue of *The New Success* Magazine.

Headline: Would You Give $1 for 16 Dancing Lessons If -

The word "If"- drags you right into the ad.

By the time you finish reading the first paragraph, the benefits you'll gain far outweigh the cost of the dance lessons.

The ad builds credibility by:

1) Telling you that Arthur Murray taught the Vanderbilts how to dance.

2) Pay no money until you receive the course.

3) If you are not completely satisfied with the course in every way, return it and Mr. Murray will return your dollar promptly without question.

Giving 16 lessons for one dollar exemplified the "loss leader" theme that worked so very well with almost every ad campaign I ever created for a client.

Would You Give $1 for 16 Dancing Lessons If —

learning to become a good dancer made you so popular that everyone would be anxious to have you attend their social affairs,—and if learning to dance the Murray Way gave you poise, ease, self-confidence and helped develop your personality,—would you be willing to pay $1 for 16 dancing lessons from America's foremost authority on social dancing?

Arthur Murray, instructor to the Vanderbilts and many other fashionable people in America and Europe, has perfected a wonderful new method by which you can learn any of the latest dance steps in a few minutes— and all of the dances in a short time.

Even if you don't know one step from another—or whether you already know some of the steps—through Arthur Murray's method you can quickly and easily master any dance without a partner and without music, right in your own home,—or the lessons won't cost you a cent. More than 60,000 have learned this new easy way. Your own success is *guaranteed*.

Do You Know

The Correct Dancing Position
How to Gain Confidence
How to Follow Successfully
How to Avoid Embarrassing Mistakes
The Art of Making Your Feet Look Attractive
The Correct Walk in the Fox Trot
The Basic Principles in Waltzing
How to Waltz Backward
The Secret of Leading
The Chasse in the Fox Trot
The Forward Waltz Step
How to Leave One Partner to Dance with Another
How to Learn and Also Teach Your Child to Dance
What the Advanced Teacher Should Know
How to Develop Your Sense of Rhythm
Etiquette of the Ballroom

Proof You Can Learn at Home in One Evening

To show you how easily any one can learn to dance at home without music or partner, Arthur Murray has consented to send, for a limited time only, his 16 Introductory Lessons for $1.00. *Don't send any money now—* just the coupon. When the postman hands you the 16-lesson course just deposit $1.00 with him, plus a few cents postage, in full payment.

Keep the course for 5 days, and if within 5 days you are not perfectly satisfied in every way, return it and Mr. Murray will return your dollar promptly without question. Learn in private—surprise your friends. Act **Now** and be a good dancer **soon**.

16 Introductory Lessons $1.00

Arthur Murray, Studio 507, 100 Fifth Avenue, N. Y.

Ad #5: Little Leather Library

The Little Leather Library Corporation was formed August 1915 by Max Sackheim and Harry Scherman.

This ad ran in the August 1916 issue of *Cosmopolitan Magazine.*

Headline: "Thirty Books Bound in Genuine Limp Leather - Only $5.75"

These literary classics practically sell themselves. However, the free bookcase and risk free trial period help give that extra push to fill out the coupon.

Remember, **WW ONE** was in full swing in 1916. Many ladies were left at home with nothing better to do with their spare time than read the classics. We chose the titles with that in mind. Strangely enough, many of those titles are still considered classics to this day.

Single Volumes 25c Each

Ad #6: Little Leather Library

This ad ran in the November 1916 issue of *Hearst's* Magazine

Headline: 60 Books - Bound in Leather - SHIPPED FREE FOR INSPECTION **$1**

That lures you into the ad before you realize that it's $1 down after 5 days if you keep the books. So you either go to the coupon to find out the total cost or you continue to read the ad.

The pure simplicity of these offers is what helped to sell over 40 million books in less than 10 years. And it was mostly done on a part-time basis.

SEND NO MONEY - pay $1 down and the rest in monthly installments. Plus you get a **free** book rack!

It doesn't matter that the total cost is nineteen dollars (and $19 in 1916 was a fair amount of money), what matters is that it's $1 down with easy to afford monthly payments. This ad is selling hard to beat terms.

Ad #7: Little Leather Library

This ad ran in the February 1921 issue of *The New Success* Magazine.

Headline: "The Greatest Bargain of My Life" - "My Brother Guessed I Paid $15 For Them"

Taken from testimonial letters - this is building high perceived value into the books.

These Little Leather Library ads are good examples of how to use illustrations effectively. Every book with easy to read titles sitting right over the $2.98 price for all 30 Masterpieces. No wasted space or unclear meanings.

The rest of the ad continues to build-up the value of these books to a level much higher than the asking price.

Under the famous SEND NO MONEY and 30 day risk free offer, take notice to the **reason- why** you had better not wait to make this purchase. If you're interested in those books, you won't wait to buy in fear of loosing this low price opportunity.

The concept of this ad (all my ads) was constructed around the chosen offer.

Ad #8: Little Leather Library

This ad ran in the May 1921 issue of *The New Success* Magazine

The concept behind this ad is similar to ad #7. The use of testimonials in a headline can be very powerful.

This is a good time to take a closer look at the order coupon.

The coupon is its own salesman. It will stand on its own. It was as true in the twenty's, as it is today, many people go right to the coupon in order to see the bottom line. If they don't like what they see, you've lost them. Make every word count.

Note that it is now 1921 and we have dropped the price even further for the first 30 books. But notice also the titles are all different, so as to capitalize on reselling to those who had already bought from the Little Leather Library before. We rarely if ever got a return for refund on these little books.

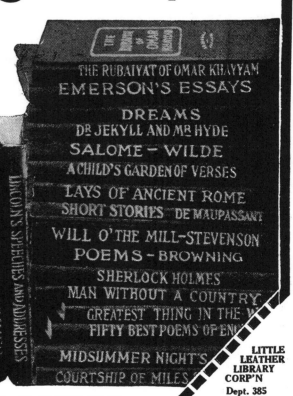

Ad #9: Little Leather Library

This SENSATION occupied a page in the October 1921 issue of *The New Success* Magazine.

The **"Send No Money"** concept has been so successful over the years that it has helped to sell many billions of dollars worth of merchandise. In fact the same concept stated differently is still being used today. **PAY NOTHING -Send for your free 30 day trial offer NOW!**

This and versions of this will continue to work as long as human nature stays the same. It overcomes the resistance to buying by making it easier to say yes than it is to say no.

Ad #10: Little Leather Library

This ad ran in the March 11, 1922 issue of the *Literary Digest*.

Is This Offer Too Good To Be True? - Curiosity grabber.

This entire ad builds honesty and credibility and it does it in a sincere tone. It does it by using **reason-why copy**. We gave reasons why this offer has been doubted by the public in the past, and how we over came that doubt to get people to try the books. This builds trust.

Using the good name of the *Literary Digest* twice in this ad, helps to build more trust.

Under the sub-headline **"What about the Price"**? - we give you the reason why the price is so low and how we can afford to do it. This increases the perceived value of the books and again builds more honesty into the ad.

Next to the coupon box are prices people have guessed that these books are worth. And they are in our records if anyone is interested in inspecting them.

"Send No Money" is the icing on the cake!

Is this offer too good to be true?

Is it possible that we are offering a value too great to be credible?
Do people shy at the thought of getting too much for their money?

WE recently mailed several thousand circulars to book-lovers. We described and pictured these thirty volumes of the Little Leather Library honestly, sincerely, accurately. But we received relatively few orders.

Then we mailed several more thousand circulars to booklovers, *this time enclosing a sample cover* of one of the volumes illustrated above. Orders came in by the hundred! The reason, we believe, is that most people can not believe we can really offer so great a value unless they *see a sample!*

In this advertisement, naturally, it is impossible for us to show you a sample volume. The best we can do is to describe and picture the books in the limited space of this page. We depend on your faith in the statements made by the advertisements appearing in Literary Digest; and we are hoping you will believe what we say, instead of thinking this offer is "too good to be true."

What this offer is

Here then is our offer. The illustration above shows thirty of the world's greatest masterpieces of literature. These include the finest works of such immortal authors as Shakespeare, Kipling, Stevenson, Emerson, Poe, Coleridge, Burns, Omar Khayyam, Macaulay, Lincoln, Washington, Oscar Wilde, Gilbert, Longfellow, Drummond, Conan Doyle, Edward Everett Hale, Thoreau, Tennyson, Browning, and others. These are books which no one cares to confess he has not read and

re-read; books which bear reading a score of times.

Each of these volumes is complete—this is not that abomination, a collection of extracts; the paper is a high-grade white wove antique, equal to that used in books selling at $1.50 to $2.00; the type is clear and easy to read; the binding is a beautiful limp material, tinted in antique copper and green, and so handsomely embossed as to give it the appearance of hand tooled leather.

And, though each of these volumes is complete, (the entire set contains over 3,000 pages) a volume can be carried conveniently wherever you go, in your pocket or purse; several can be placed in your handbag or grip; or the entire thirty can be placed on your library table "without cluttering it up" as one purchaser expressed it.

What about the price?

Producing such fine books is, in itself, no great achievement. But the aim of this enterprise has been to produce them at a price that anyone in the whole land could afford; the only way we could do this was to manufacture them in quantities of nearly a million at a time—to bring the price down through "quantity production." And we relied for our sales on our faith that Americans would rather read classics than trash. What happened? OVER TEN MILLION of these volumes have already been purchased by people in every walk of life.

Yet we know, from our daily mail, that many thousands of people still cannot believe we can sell 30 such volumes for $2.98 (plus postage). We do not know how to combat this skepticism. All we can say is: send for these 30 volumes; if you are not satisfied, return them at any time within a month and you will not be out one penny. Of the thousands of Literary Digest readers who purchased this set when we advertised it in previous issues *not one* in a hundred expressed dissatisfaction for any reason whatever.

Send No Money

No description, no illustration, can do these 30 volumes justice. You must see them. We should like to send every reader a sample, but frankly our profit is so small we cannot afford it. We offer, instead, to send the entire set on trial. Simply mail the coupon or a letter; when the set arrives, pay the postman $2.98 plus postage; then examine the books. As stated above, your money will be returned at any time within 30 days for any reason, or for NO reason, if you request it. Mail the coupon or a letter NOW while this page is before you, or you may forget.

Little Leather Library Corp'n

Dept. 263,   354 Fourth Avenue, New York

Many people who have been asked to guess the value of these books have estimated, before we told them the price, that they are worth from $50 to $100 for the complete set. These records are on file for inspection of any one interested.

Ad #11: Little Leather Library

This ad ran in the March 1923 issue of *National Geographic.*

The testimonial approach sold many little books.

The first paragraph quickly sells you on all the happy customers and the fact that twenty million books have been sold and every customer is delighted.

FREE! - four volumes of Kipling - adding to the perceived value of this offer.

Notice the use of the rider in the coupon for bumping up the dollar amount of each purchase.

"I don't see how you can do it"
"Greatest bargain of my life"
"Never received so much for the money"
"More wonderful than represented"
"These books have traveled thousands of miles with me"

HUNDREDS of pages of National Geographic Magazine could be filled with expressions even more enthusiastic than the above, from purchasers of this beautiful set of the Little Leather Library volumes. But there is a great "silent vote" even more impressive. Close to *twenty million* of the great masterpieces in this edition have already been purchased, by tens of thousands of book-lovers in every walk of life. Every volume was sold subject to 30 days' approval, under a straightforward, money-back guarantee. Twenty million books that could have been returned for refund, *but were not:* no more convincing evidence could be presented as to the extraordinary value given here!

Is this offer too good to be true?

Think of purchasing 30 volumes, including the greatest masterpieces of literature, all for only $2.98. These include the finest works of such immortal authors as Shakespeare, Kipling, Stevenson, Emerson, Poe, Coleridge, Burns, Omar Khayyam, Macaulay, Lincoln, Washington, Oscar Wilde, Gilbert, Longfellow, Drummond, Conan Doyle, Edward Everett Hale, Thoreau, Tennyson, Browning, and others. Each volume is complete, is beautifully bound in a rich, embossed Croft which looks so much like leather that even experts are often confused. The entire set *contains over 3,000 pages.* Is it surprising that even our friends among publishers wonder how it can be done? The answer is no secret; it is done simply by printing in editions of a million books at a time.

Sent on Approval

No description, no illustration, can do justice to these books. You must see them. If you are the least bit doubtful, all we can do is send this set of 30 volumes to YOU on approval. Send no money now—just the coupon or a letter. Pay only $2.98 plus postage when the set arrives—then send it back if you are even *slightly* disappointed and we will not only refund your money, but postage both ways.

LITTLE LEATHER LIBRARY CORP.
Dept. 123   354 Fourth Avenue, New York

Ad #12: Little Leather Library

This ad ran in the October 1923 issue of The *National Geographic.*

"How Can This Incredible Offer Be Made?" - along with the sub-headline, this is a curiosity grabber.

The rest of this ad is another good example of **reason-why copy.** This ad builds honesty, credibility, and it does it in a sincere way.

Whenever you make a claim or special offer in your advertising, come up with the **honest** reason-why, and then state it sincerely. You'll sell many more products this way.

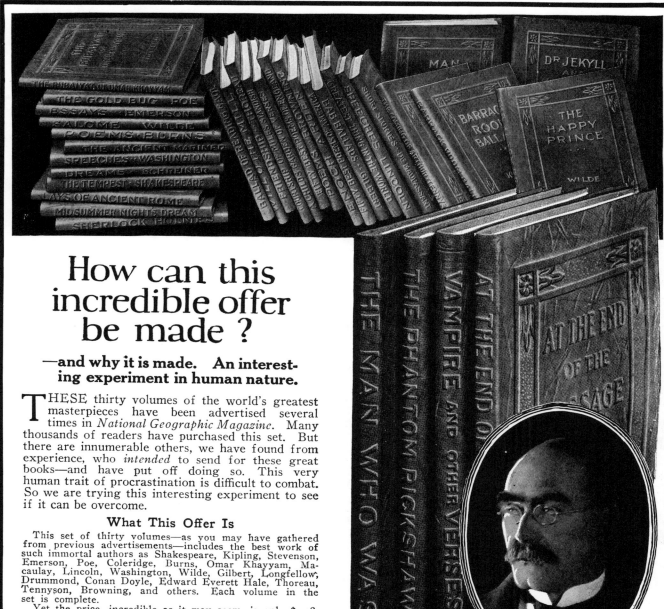

Ad #13: Little Leather Library:

This ad ran in the March 1924 issue of *National Geographic.*

The headline and sub-headline grabs your curiosity.

The first part of the ad sells you on the FREE Lincoln book ends. And the reason why we're willing to loose money on this introductory offer in order to get you to purchase this new set of 30 classics.

Another example of convincing reason-why copy.

This same concept of truthful advertising works just as well today. The more you truthfully tell, the more you'll sell.

The claims that are made **aren't** backed by **empty promises.**

An Offer That May Never Be Made Again

Why we have been willing to lose money on this introductory offer—and why it must soon be withdrawn

HERE is one of those rare bargains you are offered only once in *months.*

And this may be the *last time* it will ever be offered.

We have been willing to lose money on it, for the very interesting reason explained below. Our loss, however, is *your gain.*

On this offer you are given a pair of Abraham Lincoln Book-Ends, ABSOLUTELY FREE. These book-ends are made of heavy bronzed metal, with Lincoln's head in bas-relief. They are an adornment to any library table. They would cost, if obtainable in stores, $1.00 to $1.50.

Yet they are given free—in order to introduce the NEW set of thirty Little Leather Library world's masterpieces.

We know what has happened in the past on our previous sets after they were introduced—*orders poured in by the thousands.*

The wisest thing we could do, therefore, was to introduce this NEW set QUICKLY into representative homes. We know what will happen after this is done. Every set will become a "silent salesman," more powerful than any other form of advertising we could do.

That is the reason—the only reason—we have been willing to lose money on this offer.

This NEW set is, in many respects, the finest we have ever published. It includes the *best works,* each one complete, of such

famous authors as:

Barrie	Irving
Kipling	Ibsen
Shaw	Shakespeare
Yeats	Lamb
Allen	Moore
Balzac	Tennyson
Browning	Plato
Eliz. Browning	Wilde
Dumas	Maeterlinck
Emerson	Turgenev
Whitman	Longfellow
Whittier	Dante
Poe	Elbert Hubbard

These thirty volumes, *without* the book-ends, have been valued (by hundreds of people who were asked to guess) *at from five to fifteen times their price.* Each volume is complete. The binding is a beautiful limp Croftcott, handsomely embossed, and tinted an antique copper and green, so that even experts have mistaken it for hand-tooled leather. *The paper is actually the same quality as that used in books that sell regularly for $2.00 apiece.* Yet the price,

for *all thirty* volumes, is only $2.98.

How can *thirty such books* be sold for only $2.98? Simply by printing in editions of *at least one million books at a time,* relying on the good taste of the public to keep the enterprise self-sustaining. Quantity production—that is the whole secret.

Surely, sooner or later, you will want to obtain this wonderful set—at least a year's good reading for the price of a theater ticket! Why, then, not obtain it at once, taking advantage of the exceptional "premium" now offered for introductory purposes only?

Sent for Thirty Days' Examination

Do not send any money. Simply mail the coupon or a letter mentioning this advertisement. When the books and book-ends arrive, give the postman only $2.98, plus the few pennies for delivery charges. Then, if you wish, examine the books for thirty days. If you are disappointed in the slightest respect, if you do not agree that this is one of the most satisfactory purchases you have ever made, send the set back any time within the thirty days, and your money will instantly be refunded. Can a fairer offer be made? References: Manufacturers' Trust Company, or any magazine. NOTE: When the present supply of book-ends is gone this offer will be withdrawn. It is made for introductory purposes only. If you want to take advantage of it, it is advisable NOT TO DELAY. Mail coupon or letter at once.

Little Leather Library Corporation
Dept. 123
218 West 40th Street   New York, N. Y.

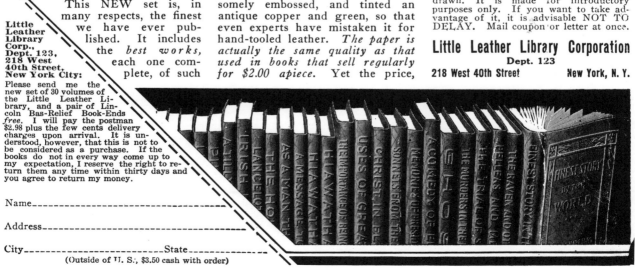

Ad #14: Book-of-the-Month Club

This ad ran in the July 1927 issue of *The Atlantic Monthly.*

The Book-of-the-Month Club News - FREE.

If you are a book-lover, this two step method would surely have got you. Real book-lovers can't get enough information about books.

Many of today's businesses are adopting this idea of a free newsletter to gain inquiries. It can work very well provided you have information that has news value.

What's the *"book-of-the-month"* this month—and why?

Let us send you—free—the current issue of
THE BOOK-OF-THE-MONTH CLUB NEWS

THIS is a fascinating little publication, part of the service given by the Book-of-the-Month Club to its subscribers. Send for the current issue. Learn what book the judges of the Book-of-the-Month Club selected, this month, as the "book-of-the-month." Read their interesting reasons for the choice. Read also the extremely illuminating reports upon other new and important books, just out. The judges of the Book-of-the-Month Club are: Henry Seidel Canby, chairman; Heywood Broun, Dorothy Canfield, Christopher Morley and William Allen White. Over forty thousand of the most notable people in the country, judicious and perspicacious readers like yourself, now use the service of the Book-of-the-Month Club to make sure they will "keep up with the best new books." It absolutely prevents you from missing the new books you are anxious to read. Yet this service, unique, valuable and convenient though it is, does not cost you one cent. You pay only for the books you take, and the same price as if you got them from the publisher himself—by mail. You owe it to yourself *at least* to find out how this unique service works. Mail the coupon below. The current issue of the *News* will be sent to you, absolutely without any obligation.

*Handed to you by the postman—
the books you don't want to miss*

Ad #15: Book-of-the-Month Club

This ad ran in the January 1929 issue of *The Review of Reviews*.

These ads created a feeling of becoming part of an elite literary group. A group that not only received information about the best books, but they gained the privilege of getting this information first, before anyone else. Not to mention the Selecting Committee (critics) that will save you time in picking out the right books for you!

What's the "book-of-the-month" this month ~ and why?

IT is a very remarkable new book, not yet published, chosen by the distinguished group of five critics who compose our Selecting Committee, as the outstanding work among the many books that were submitted last month, *in advance of publication*, by the publishers of this country.

If you were a subscriber to the Book-of-the-Month Club service, you would not only receive a full report about this book, but you would make sure of getting it, if you decided after reading our Committee's report, that it was a book you would not care to miss reading.

You would not be *obliged* to take it, however, unless it appealed to you. You are given the opportunity of choosing some other important forthcoming book. For instance, last month there were some twenty books about which our Committee reported to members. You might have preferred one of these, in place of the "book-of-the-month;" and if none of them appealed to you—you would not have had to take any!

Moreover, if you take any one of the Books recommended by our Committee, and find you have been misled by the report, *you may exchange it for another at the same price.* This "guarantee of satisfaction" completely protects you in your book purchases.

Through this unique and complete service, you need never miss any book you are particularly keen to read. How often now, through oversight, do you forget to obtain outstanding books you intend to read, and then have to confess, months afterwards, that "you never got around to it?"

Over 90,000 of the most notable people in the country—in every line of endeavor—now guard themselves against missing the new books they want to read, by belonging to the Book-of-the-Month Club. They are people of your tastes and standards. They don't receive any book, unless they want it; but they do make absolutely sure, by this service, *that they get and read the books they are anxious not to miss.*

Why not try it yourself? The service does not cost you anything! There are no dues, no fees, no extra charges of any kind. *You pay only for the books you decide to take,* and the same price as if you got them from the publisher himself by mail!

Surely, among the 150 or more books our Committee will report upon in 1929, there will be several you will be very anxious not to miss. Find out how this valuable service will absolutely prevent you from missing them. Mail the coupon below for full information. Your request will involve you in no obligation.

Henry Seidel Canby
Chairman

Heywood
Broun

Dorothy
Canfield

Christopher
Morley

William Allen
White

THE SELECTING COMMITTEE OF THE BOOK-OF-THE-MONTH CLUB

Ad #16: Pelton Publishing Company - The Power of Will

This ad was written between the years 1915-1917 by Maxwell Sackheim while employed by Ruthrauff & Ryan. As Max stated years ago:

> The Pelton ads were, in my opinion, the beginning of a copy era at Ruthrauff & Ryan that had a great deal to do with revolutionizing advertising, not only in the mail order field but also in other areas.

Headline:
" How it Feels to Earn $1000 a Week." - By a Young Man Who Four Years Ago Drew a $25 a Week Salary. Tells How He Accomplished it.

That headline is the beginning of a human interest approach that sold a lot of books.

You'll benefit by reading the rest of the ad.

How it Feels to Earn $1000 a Week

By a Young Man Who Four Years Ago Drew a $25 a Week Salary. Tells How He Accomplished It.

How does it feel to earn $1000 a week? How does it feel to have earned $200,000 in four years? How does it feel to be free from money worries? How does it feel to have everything one can want? These are questions I shall answer for the benefit of my reader out of my own personal experience. And I shall try to explain, simply and clearly the secret of what my friends call my phenomenal success.

Let me begin four years ago. At that time my wife and I and our two babies were living on my earnings of twenty-five dollars a week. We occupied a tiny flat, wore the simplest clothes, had to be satisfied with the cheapest entertainment—and dreamed sweet dreams of the time when I should be earning fifty dollars a week. That was the limit of my ambition. Indeed, it seemed to be the limit of my possibilities. For I was but an average man, without influential friends, without a liberal education, without a dominating personality, and without money.

With nothing to begin with, I have become the sole owner of a business which has paid me over $200,000 in clear profits during the past four years and which now pays me more than a thousand dollars a week. I did not gamble. I did not make my money in Wall Street. My business is not a war baby—on the contrary, many others in my line have failed since the war began.

In four years, the entire scheme of my life has changed. Instead of living in a two by four flat, we occupy our own home, built for us at a cost of over $60,000. We have three automobiles. Our children go to private schools. We have everything we want, and we want the best of everything. Instead of dreaming of fifty dollars a week I am dreaming in terms of a million dollars—with greater possibilities of my dream coming true than my former dream of earning fifty dollars a week.

What brought about this remarkable change? What transformed me, almost overnight, from a slow-going, easily-satisfied, average man—into a positive, quick-acting, determined individual who admits no defeat, who overcomes every obstacle, and who completely dominates every situation? It all began with a question my wife asked me one evening after reading an article in a magazine about a great engineer who was said to earn a $50,000 salary.

"How do you suppose it feels to earn $1000 a week?" she asked. And without thinking, I replied "I haven't the slightest idea, my dear, so the only way to find out is to *earn it.*" We both laughed, and soon the question was apparently forgotten.

But that night, and for weeks afterward, the same question *and my reply* kept popping into my brain. I began to analyze the qualities of the successful men in our town. What is it that enables them to get everything they want? They are not better educated than I—indeed, some are far less intelligent. But they must have possessed some quality that I lacked. Perhaps it was their mental attitude; perhaps they look at things from an entirely different angle than I. Whatever it was, that "something" was the secret of their success. It was the one thing that placed them head and shoulders above me in money-earning ability. In all other ways we were the same.

Determined to find out what that vital spark of success was, I bought books on every subject that pertained to the mind. I followed one idea after another. But I didn't seem to get anywhere. Finally, when almost discouraged, I came across a copy of "Power of Will." Like a bolt out of a clear sky there flashed in my brain the secret I had been seeking. There was the real, fundamental principle of all success—Power of Will. There was the brain faculty I lacked, and which every successful man possesses.

"Power of Will" was written by Prof. Frank Channing Haddock, a scientist, whose name ranks with such leaders of thought as James, Bergson and Royce. After twenty years of research and study, he had completed the most thorough and constructive study of will power ever made. I was astonished to read his statement that, "The will is just as susceptible of development as the muscles of the body!" And Dr. Haddock had actually set down the very rules, lessons and exercises by which anyone could develop the will, making it a bigger, stronger force each day, simply through an easy, progressive course of training.

It is almost needless to say that I at once began to practice the exercises formulated by Dr. Haddock. And I need not recount the extraordinary results that I obtained almost from the first day. Shortly after that, I took hold of a business that for twelve years had been losing money. I started with $300 of borrowed capital. During my first year I made $30,000. My second year paid me $50,000. My third year netted me $70,000. Last year, due to increased costs of materials, my profits were only $50,000, though my volume of business increased. New plans which I am forcing through, will bring my profits for the present fiscal year up to $65,000.

Earning a thousand dollars a week makes me feel secure against want. It gives me the money with which to buy whatever will make my family happy. It enables me to take a chance on an investment that looks good, without worrying about losing the money. It frees my mind of financial worries. It has made me healthier, more contented, and keener minded. It is the greatest recipe I know for happiness.

Prof. Haddock's lessons, rules and exercises in will training have recently been compiled and published in book form by the Pelton Publishing Co., of Meriden, Conn. I am authorized to say that any reader who cares to examine the book may do so without sending any money in advance. In other words, if after five days' reading, you do not feel that the book is worth $3, the sum asked, return it and you will owe nothing. When you receive your copy for examination I suggest that you first read the articles on the law of great thinking; how to develop analytical power; how to perfectly concentrate on any subject; how to guard against errors in thought; how to drive from the mind unwelcome thoughts; how to develop fearlessness; how to use the mind in sickness; how to acquire a dominating personality.

Never before have business men and women needed this help so badly as in these trying times. Hundreds of real and imaginary obstacles confront us every day, and only those who are masters of themselves and who hold their heads up, will succeed. "Power of Will" as never before, is an absolute necessity—an investment in self-culture which no one can afford to deny himself.

Some few doubters will scoff at the idea of will power being the fountainhead of wealth, position and everything we are striving for. But the great mass of intelligent men and women will at least investigate for themselves by sending for the book at the publisher's risk. I am sure that any book that has done for me—and for thousands of others—what "Power of Will" has done—is well worth investigating. It is interesting to note that among the 250,000 owners of "Power of Will" are such prominent men as Supreme Court Justice Parker; Wu Ting Fang, Ex-U. S. Chinese Ambassador; Lieut.-Gov. McKelvie, of Nebraska; Assistant Postmaster-General Britt; General Manager Christeson, of Wells-Fargo Express Co.; E. St. Elmo Lewis; Governor Arthur Capper of Kansas, and thousands of others. In fact, today "Power of Will" is just as important, and as necessary to a man's or woman's equipment for success, as a dictionary. To try to succeed without Power of Will is like trying to do business without a telephone.

As your first step in will training, I suggest immediate action in this matter before you. It is not even necessary to write a letter. Use the form below, if you prefer, addressing it to the Pelton Publishing Company, 47-R Wilcox Block, Meriden, Conn., and the book will come by return mail. This one act may mean the turning point of your life, as it has meant to me and to so many others.

The cost of paper, printing and binding has almost doubled during the past three years, in spite of which "Power of Will" has not been increased in price. The publisher feels that so great a work should be kept as low-priced as possible, but in view of the enormous increase in the cost of every manufacturing item, the present edition will be the last sold at the present price. The next edition will cost more. I urge you to send in the coupon now.

Ad #17: The Tulloss School of Touch Typing

This ad ran in the October 1915 issue of *Metropolitan.*

Max was involved with writing this ad while with Ruthrauff & Ryan.

There's an interesting story behind this ad. When Ruthrauff & Ryan first got the Tulloss account, the course was being sold as the "Tulloss System of Touch Typing" with little success. After doing some research on why the course was unsuccessful, it was soon discovered that most touch typists didn't have much faith in touch typing courses. The reason they had so little faith was because the touch typing courses offered in the colleges weren't very helpful. So the course was renamed **"The New Way in Typewriting."**

The campaign was a huge success. It proved how powerful the word **"NEW"** was as an advertising attraction. That word, of course, is still as powerful today.

Ad #18: The Pelman Institute of America

Pelman institute was another Sackheim & Scherman correspondence school account. The correspondence course was imported from England.

Maxwell Sackheim wrote this ad in 1927.

Notice the editorial form of the layout.

Scatter-brained!

No wonder he never accomplishes anything worthwhile!

Sir Harry Lauder, Comedian.   Baroness Orczy, Author.
W. L. George, Author.   Prince Charles of Sweden.

HIS mind is a hodge-podge of half-baked ideas. He thinks of a thousand "schemes" to make money quickly—but DOES nothing about ANY of them.

Thoughts flash into and out of his brain with the speed of lightning. New ideas rush in pell-mell, crowding out old ones before they have taken form or shape.

He is SCATTER-BRAINED.

His mind is like a powerful automobile running wild—destroying his hopes, his dreams, his POSSIBILITIES!

He wonders why he does not get ahead. He cannot understand why others, with less ability, pass him in the prosperity parade.

He pities himself, excuses himself, sympathizes with himself.

And the great tragedy is that he has every quality that leads to success—intelligence, originality, imagination, ambition.

His trouble is that he does not know how to USE his brain.

His mental make-up needs an overhauling.

There are millions like him—failures, half-successes—slaves to those with BALANCED, ORDERED MINDS.

It is a known fact that most of us use only one-tenth of our brain power. The other nine-tenths is dissipated into thousands of fragmentary thoughts, in day dreaming, in wishing.

We are paid for ONE-TENTH of what we possess because that is all we USE. We are hundred horse-power motors delivering only TEN horse power.

What can be done about it?

The reason most people fall miserably below what they dream of attaining in life is that certain mental faculties in them BECOME ABSOLUTELY ATROPHIED THROUGH DISUSE, just as a muscle often does.

If, for instance, you lay for a year in bed, you would sink to the ground when you arose; your leg muscles, UNUSED FOR SO LONG, could not support you.

It is no different with those rare mental faculties which you envy others for possessing. You actually DO possess them, but they are ALMOST ATROPHIED, like unused muscles, simply because they are faculties you seldom, if ever, USE.

Be honest with yourself. You know in your heart that you have failed, failed miserably, to attain what you once dreamed of.

Was that fine ambition unattainable? OR WAS THERE JUST SOMETHING WRONG WITH YOU? Analyze yourself, and you will see that at bottom THERE WAS A WEAKNESS SOMEWHERE IN YOU.

What WAS the matter with you?

Find out by means of Pelmanism; then develop the particular mental faculty that you lack. You CAN develop it easily; Pelmanism will show you just how; 550,000 Pelmanists, MANY OF WHOM WERE HELD BACK BY YOUR VERY PROBLEM, will tell you that this is true.

Among those who advocate Pelmanism are:

T. P. O'Connor, "Father of the House of Commons."

The late Sir H. Rider Haggard, Famous Novelist.

General Sir Robert Baden-Powell, Founder of the Boy Scout Movement.

Judge Ben B. Lindsey, Founder of the Juvenile Court, Denver.

Frank P. Walsh, Former Chairman of National War Labor Board.

Jerome K. Jerome, Novelist.

Gen. Sir Frederick Maurice, Director of Military Operations, Imperial General Staff.

Admiral Lord Beresford, G.C.B., G.C.V.O.

—and others, of equal prominence, too numerous to mention here.

Pelmanism is the science of applied psychology, which has swept the world with the force of a religion. It has awakened powers in individuals, all over the world, they did not DREAM they possessed.

A remarkable book called "Scientific Mind Training" has been written about Pelmanism. IT CAN BE OBTAINED FREE. Yet thousands of people who read this announcement and who NEED this book will not send for it. "It's no use," they will say. "It will do me no good," they will tell themselves. "It's all tommyrot," others will say.

But if they use their HEADS they will realize that people cannot be HELPED by tommyrot and that there MUST be something in Pelmanism, when it has such a record behind it, and when it is endorsed by the kind of people listed here.

If you are made of the stuff that isn't content to remain a slave—if you have taken your last whipping from life,—if you have a spark of INDEPENDENCE left in your soul, write for this free book. It tells you what Pelmanism is, WHAT IT HAS DONE FOR OTHERS, and what it can do for you.

The first principle of YOUR success is to do something definite in your life. You cannot afford to remain undecided, vascilating, day-dreaming, for you will soon again sink into the mire of discouragement. Let Pelmanism help you FIND YOURSELF Mail the coupon below now—while your resolve to DO SOMETHING ABOUT YOURSELF is strong.

THE PELMAN INSTITUTE OF AMERICA

Approved as a correspondence school under the laws of the State of New York

19 West 44th St.   Suite 512   New York City

The Pelman Institute of America,
19 West 44th St., Suite 512
New York City.

I want you to show me what Pelmanism has actually done for over 550,000 people. Please send me your free book, "Scientific Mind Training." This places me under no obligation whatever.

Name.....................................

Address.................................

City.......................... State................

Ad # 19: Old Trusty Incubators

Maxwell Sackheim was involved with writing this ad some time between the years 1905 to 1912 while employed with Long-Critchfield Corporation in Chicago.

The American standard of living is due in no small measure to the imaginative genius of advertising. It not only increases buyer demand by its impact upon the competitive process, but it stimulates the constant quest of improvement of product quality.

-- Adlai Stevenson

PRESS
INFORMATION

TM

FROM: Roberta Wexler
DIRECT MARKETING ASSOCIATION, INC.
6 EAST 43RD STREET, NEW YORK, N.Y 10017
PHONE: 212/689-4977

FOR IMMEDIATE RELEASE
October 21, 1983

Maxwell Sackheim

Named To DMA Hall Of Fame

Miami Beach, Oct. 21, 1983 -- The late Maxwell Sackheim, founder of the Book-of-the-Month Club, was named today to the Direct Marketing Association's Hall of Fame. The award was announced during DMA's Annual Conference which has attracted over 5000 people from the rapidly-growing $135 billion direct marketing field.

Maxwell Sackheim, who died in 1982, and was founder of the Book-of-the-Month Club and the "Negative option technique," left an indelible mark on direct mail and direct response advertising in a career which spanned over 60 years. After serving as president of an agricultural mail order business from 1928-44, he returned to advertising in 1946 and formed the Maxwell Sackheim & Co. agency. His client roster included the literary Guild, Famous Artists schools, Young People's

Records and Time, Inc.

Many of his favorite and most successful campaigns, including the launching of the American Express credit card, were documented in his book, "My First 65 Years in Advertising", published in 1975. His favorite opening when called on to give a speech was, "Can you see me?" Although small in physical stature, he was a giant in influence among his peers.

Mr. Sackheim's two sons, Robert and Sherman accepted the Hall of Fame Award honoring their father.

The Hall of Fame, established by DMA in 1978, "as a permanent recognition of individuals who have made major contributions to the theory and practice of direct mail or direct marketing," has 23 members. They include Leon L. Bean, John Caples, Reuben H. Donnelley, Lester Wunderman, Richard W. Sears and Aaron Montgomery Ward.

DMA is the oldest and largest trade association in the field of direct marketing, with over 2,300 corporate members in the United States and 37 other countries.

Billion Dollar Marketing
CONCEPTS AND APPLICATIONS

BOOK THREE

Maxwell Sackheim's

History of

Advertising

Maxwell Sackheim's
History Of Advertising

One of the pet theories about advertising has been that the consumer should be kept unaware of its existence. The effect should be on the subconscious rather than the conscious. Like the background music for a movie, it's at its best when you don't seem to hear it but it is there for you to absorb subliminally.

It can't be ignored.

Today we are so completely surrounded by advertising that to ignore the public's interest in it would be to hide one's head in the sand, ostrich-fashion! It can't be ignored. Youngsters know the songs for television and radio commercials better than they know the faces of casual friends. And the development of advertising methods continues in technological and psychological effectiveness.

Experiments have even been made to project advertising messages in color, against the background of clouds. You may yet be reminded to take "A break today" or stock up on your favorite brand of breakfast cereal every time you gaze toward a sunset or a full moon, provided it can be determined who has the right to use those clouds and maybe more important, how many artificial clouds can be created by machine for advertising purposes.

It is almost certain that someday advertising slogans will come bouncing down at us from the man-launched satellites circling the globe. And since advertising is no longer the private property of the professionals, and is actually in the public domain, you'll be interested in some of its early history.

The first known written advertisement came from Egypt -- a 3000 year-old papyrus, inscribed with the following message:

The man slave Shem having run away from his good master, Hapu, the Weaver, all good citizens of Thebes are enjoined to help return him. He is a Hittite, 5'2" tall, of ruddy complexion and brown eyes. For news of his whereabouts half a gold coin is offered. And for his return to the shop of Hapu, the Weaver, where the best cloth is woven to your desire, a whole gold coin is offered.

Even 3000 years ago, the advertising of extra incentives was recognized as a factor in speeding up "sales."

So, you see, even 3000 years ago, the advertising of extra incentives was recognized as a factor in speeding up "sales."

Then came the age of town criers. The Greeks called attention to the sale of slaves or cattle and made other public announcements through the "broadcasting" of the day, now identified as radio and television commercials. This one is said to have been used in ancient Athens:

> For eyes that are shining, for cheeks like the dawn;
> For beauty that lasts after girlhood is gone;   For prices in reason, the woman who knows, will buy her cosmetics from Ecko-Tic-Toes.

That spiel is better than some we hear today!

I could never find out who Ecko-Tic-Toes was but the spiel is better than some we hear today! In Rome, Carthage and years later in England, these town criers or shop barkers were employed to make known the wares and services of merchants, money-lenders and others who wished the public's patronage.

During the middle ages buyers and sellers usually met at stalls in market places, at fairs, or in shops. Professional criers were hired by the traders and selling depended upon the lungs and blarney of the crier. One can imagine the din in the market place with criers trying to out-shout each other. In "shopping streets", obstructions often were placed to check the traffic and collect a captive audience. These were known as "customer traps" and if the shoppers did not haggle and bargain they were robbed. Prices fluctuated hourly according to the customer's character and ability to pay.

Vocal advertising continued to be popular for many years. Long after other advertising methods were introduced, this peddler's cry was still heard in many neighborhoods of New York:

> Clams! Clams! My clams I want to sell today, the
> best clams of Rockaway.

In Philadelphia an elderly lady used to sit in front of a toy shop and greet home going theater crowds with her shrill invitation to:

> buy lavender at two cents a cup.

And old timers who were raised in crowded cities recall the cry of:

> any rags, any bones, any bottles today?

Even Shakespeare in "The Winter's Tale" gave a player this commercial to recite:

> Gloves as sweet as damask roses
> Masks for faces and for noses
> Pin and poking sticks of steel
> What maids lack from head to heel
> Come buy of me, come buy, come buy
> Buy, lads, or else your lasses cry.

This form of visual advertising was displayed everywhere.

After vocal advertising came sign advertising. This form of visual advertising was displayed everywhere -- even outside the bawdy houses of Pompeii, 2000 years ago. Some are still there, pointed out to men tourists only, surreptitiously, by the leering guides. In Rome, the picture of a goat was the sign of a dairy. A Mule driving a millwheel designated a bakery. A boy being whipped was the ancient sign of a school. The three golden balls still seen over pawn shop doors had their origin during the Crusades in the Eleventh Century. The first cigar store Indian, carved in London by ship carpenters, became the tobacconist's advertisement.

During the 14th and 15th Centuries few people could read the alphabet, so colors and symbols were used to relate to families, crafts and trade associations. It was universally accepted throughout Christendom as the science of heraldry. A graphic vocabulary was built up with the various hues, lines and symbols. These symbols included birds, beasts, fishes, dragons, flowers, trees wreaths, towers, turrets, ships, shoes, chain and keys, etc. The association of the colors and symbols gave information about families, merchants, guilds and companies. The ivy bush was a common tavern sign and inspired one of the earliest criticisms of advertising:

> Vino vendibili hedera non opus est -- Good wine
> needs no bush.

In the early 1600's signs were posted everywhere, even in the middle aisle of St. Paul's Church in London, where attorneys and other professional men vied with seamstresses, money-lenders and shopkeepers for business.

The Romans erected buildings and left white squares on the walls for residents to advertise their occupations and professions.

An anonymous writer recorded some of the strange associations of names and symbols in the following verse:

> I'm amazed at the Signs
> As I pass through the Town
> To see the odd mixture:
> A Magpie and Crown,
> The Whale and the Crow,
> The Razor and Hen,
> The Leg and Seven Stars,
> The Axe and the Bottle,
> The Tun and the Lute,
> The Eagle and Child,
> The Shovel and Boot.

With that advertisement,
a new phase of the
industry was born --
in-print advertising.

The very first newspaper advertisement, according to one researcher, appeared in England in a publication called *Mercurious Britannicus*, dated February 1, 1626. It was an ad for a book, which certainly must have become a best seller of the time and probably would have been the Book-of-the-Month Club's selection for that month, had the Club existed then. With that advertisement, a new phase of the industry was born -- in-print advertising. And to think, that was only six short years after the Pilgrims landed on Plymouth Rock.

In a copy of the *London Public Adviser* of May 26, 1657 we find an ad for a new beverage called COFFEE:

> It is a very wholesome and physical drink, which has many excellent virtues, closes the orifices of the stomach, fortifies the heat within, helpeth digestion, quickeneth the spirits, maketh the heart lightsum, is good against eyesores, coughs, colds, headache, dropsie, gout, scurvy, King's Evil and many others.

Coffee, tea and tobacco all appeared in Europe, first as imported wonder drugs noted for their healing powers. Queen Elizabeth sold a state monopoly in patent medicines; George III gave a testimonial for Ching's Patent Worm Lozenges.

In 1660 the first dentifrice advertisement appeared -- perhaps the first such to name a product and tell where it could be purchased. It proclaimed:

> Most excellent and improved Dentifrice to scour and cleanse the teeth, making them white as ivory, preserves from the toothache, fastens the Teeth, sweetens the Breath, and preserves the Gums and Mouth from Cankers. Made by Robert Tumer, Gentleman, and the right only are to be had at Thomas Rookes, Stationer at the East End of St. Paul's Church, near the School. The reader is desired to beware of Counterfeits.

That last line is an admonition so familiar to us these days.

In the early 1700's *The Spectator* in London became a much sought-after advertising medium. The first issue had a print order of 3,000 and later as much as 30,000. It was filled with personal notices, houses for sale or rent, dry goods ads, book ads, financial schemes, articles lost or stolen, the apprehension of deserters, as well as ads for tobacco, tea, lotteries, wigs, auction sales and, of course, medicine to cure every ailment.

The first successful newspaper in America was *The Boston News Letter*. It carried this announcement in 1704:

> This News-Letter is to be continued Weekly, and all persons who have Houses, Lands Tenements, Farms, Shoppes, Vessels, Goods, Wares or Merchandise, etc. to be Sold or Let, or servants Run-Away or Goods Stole or Lost may have the same Reasonable Rates from Twelve Pence to Five Shillings.

That announcement brought in the very first paid advertisement in a print-periodical which ran May 8, 1704, and asked for a buyer or renter for an Oyster Bay, Long Island estate.

Advertising was becoming so widespread that in 1758, Dr. Samuel Johnson wrote:

> Advertisements are now so numerous that they are now negligently perused and it is therefore become necessary to gain attention by magnificence of promise and by eloquence sometimes sublime and sometimes pathetic.

Samuel Johnson's remark identified advertising with active persuasion.

It was through the columns of newspapers that the word "advertisement" acquired its generic significance. Dr. Johnson's remark identified advertising with active persuasion, but just over 20 years earlier, it was defined in the second edition of Bailey's Dictionary (1736) as: "Warning only, Information, Intelligence given to persons invested in an affair; also advice, a putting in mind." To advertise was "to warn, to give Notice, Advice or Intelligence of."

George Washington turned to advertising for his needs.

George Washington turned to advertising for his needs, printing and distributing posters and handbills to recruit able-bodied men for his army. In the same era, the *Boston Gazette* of December 11, 1768 carried an advertisement for false teeth made by Paul Revere, who long before his midnight ride was famous for his skill as a mechanical dentist. He advertised:

> Whereas many persons are so unfortunate as to lose their Fore-Teeth by accident, and otherways, to their great detriment, not only in looks but speaking, both in Public and Private: This is to inform all such, that they may have them replaced with Artificial Ones that look as well as the natural, by Paul Revere, Goldsmith, near the Head of Dr. Clark's Wharef, Boston.

For the do-it-yourselfers, there was this ad:

> TEETH
> are easily and painlessly filled at home without previous experience by using Dr. Hale's Home Dental Outfit and Method. It prevents toothache and early loss by stopping the cause, and secures perfect, permanent teeth. Every article in the outfit is warranted to be first-class. Money promptly refunded if unsatisfactory. Price $3.00 and $5.00, with full directions, post-paid.
> NATIONAL DENTAL SUPPLY CO.,
> 42 Warren St., Boston, Mass.

Thomas Fleming, historian, wrote "it is clear from reading the advertisements of 1776 shopkeepers that they were appealing to a wealthy public. They offered a staggering array of dress materials: Flowered, striped, figured and plain modes and satins in every

193

imaginable color, equally numerous colors of damask, saracenet and lustring, luxurious Chinese taffetas, cotton chintzes and calicoes from India and linen from Ireland and Russia. A good complexion was considered a necessity. There were paints from China, a lip salve from India, etc. The Bloom of Circasia instantly gave to the cheek a rose hue not to be distinguished from the animated bloom or rural beauty. Moreover it was guaranteed not to come off with perspiration. Other popular items were Jerusalem wash balls and 'swan skin and silk powder puffs,' almond paste for the hands and face, and a wide variety of perfumes, which were badly needed because frequent bathing was not in fashion."

The Times predicted that advertising would have to be more responsible.

In 1788 *The Times* predicted that advertising in newspapers would have to be more responsible, and published a far-sighted statement ending:

> To indecent language or double entendre, no place shall be given in THE TIMES, nor shall it contain any passage capable of insulting the eye or ear or modesty or suffusing the cheek of innocence with a blush.

Consumers learned to be wary and it was only after the Quakers established fixed prices for merchandise that trading could result in a fairly honest fashion. However, old suspicions die hard. But eventually shopkeepers with permanent places of business and a sense of responsibility courted their customers and won their confidence.

Perhaps one of the first American advertisers still dominant in commerce today is the Colgate Company which made soap and candles in New York. In 1817 they offered for sale, as they said:

> on best terms, a constant supply of soap, Mould and Dipt Candles of the first quality.

I've featured an old Colgate perfume ad on the following page.

These three bottles contained three of the most popular imported perfumes

These three bottles were filled with domestic perfumes made by Colgate & Co.

Which would you have chosen in this Perfume Test?

THE test was made by 103 representative women, comparing six perfumes—three of which were the most popular foreign perfumes and three were domestic, made by Colgate & Co. Over ⅗ of the 103 women chose Colgate's in preference to the imported. Before making the test 61 of the 103 said they preferred a foreign perfume, yet when the influence of a foreign label was removed 41 of these 61, or ⅔ of them, chose Colgate's first.

Every woman will be interested in the story of this test

It shows very clearly that selecting a perfume because it has a foreign label does not necessarily result in a woman's getting what she really prefers.

The test was conducted as follows by two impartial judges (Mr. F. N. Doubleday of Doubleday, Page & Co.; Mr. S. Keith Evans of the Woman's Home Companion). They purchased three of the most popular imported perfumes and three Colgate perfumes—all in original unopened bottles. The judges poured the perfumes into six plain bottles, numbered from one to six, and kept a record by which they alone knew which number represented each perfume. From time to time strips of Perfumers' Blotting Paper were scented from the numbered bottles under the supervision of the judges, and these were used in making the test. The 103 women represented business women, the stage, the

---

This is the Way They Chose

First choice of 28 women, Colgate's Florient
First choice of 26 women, Colgate's Splendor
First choice of 18 women, Foreign Perfume 4
First choice of 12 women, Foreign Perfume 2
First choice of 10 women, Foreign Perfume 5
First choice of 9 women, Colgate's Eclat

Note these little stories of women who had been buying a label rather than a perfume:

A prominent actress, who had previously used a certain French Perfume, which happened to be in this test, placed that perfume *fourth* and Florient first.

A prominent member of the senior class of Vassar College chose Colgate's Florient although what she *thought* was her favorite perfume was in this test, and accorded that perfume fifth place.

Three Smith College girls in like manner passed by their unlabeled *avowed* choice and two chose Splendor, one Éclat.

An editor of a well-known woman's periodical, whose profession brings her in touch with all that is best in perfumes, foreign or domestic, chose Colgate's Splendor after expressing a preference for a famous French perfume included in the test, which she put in second place.

---

editorial staffs of two women's magazines and college women. Each was asked to name the perfume she was in the habit of using and was then given 6 strips of the scented paper numbered 1 to 6 corresponding to the numbers on the bottles. She was asked to make a first choice, a second, a third, etc. Record was kept of *all* selections.

When the tests were completed the judges took the record, and inserted the names of the perfumes in place of the numbers from the key which they alone had. The result was then announced to Colgate & Co. It was a daring test—inspired by the confidence which we had in the superiority of our perfumes. How is your choice of perfumes determined? By what you really prefer or by a foreign label? Is it not possible that a domestic label is keeping you from the enjoyment of the particular perfume you would naturally select?

Would You like to make the Test for yourself?

If so, we will send you three Perfumers' Testing Strips, three miniature vials of the Colgate Perfumes—Florient, Splendor and Eclat—and an extra strip of paper so that you can make a comparison between Colgate's and the perfume which you may now be using.

This test will not only be valuable to you but can be used as an interesting form of entertainment for your friends. We will send full instructions as to how to make the test. Your name and address and a 2c stamp for mailing will receive prompt attention.

Write today for details showing how to make the test yourself

COLGATE & CO., Perfume Contest, Dept. 45, 199 Fulton Street, New York

Patent medicine was responsible for the rapid growth of advertising from 1840 to the outbreak of the Civil War, although the extravagant claims gave advertising a bad reputation. A cough medicine promised:

> Consumption of all sorts, radically cured by famous Elixir; It absolutely retrieves the patient though reduced to meer skeleton, quickly takes off the symptoms, as cough, hoarseness, wheezing, shortness of breath soreness of the stomach, throat or windpipe, fever, etc. Perfectly cures all internal ulcers, rectifying diseases of the stomach, creating an appetite and procuring a good digestion.

And at about the same time tobacco was described as:

It makes a man sober that was drunk.

> a cure for the gout in the feet ... it helps all sorts of agues ... it makes a man sober that was drunk ... it refreshes a weary man and yet makes a man hungry ... being taken when they go to bed, it makes one sleep soundly, and yet being taken when a man is sleepie and drowsie, it will waken his brain and quicken his industrie.

N.W. Ayer & Son, one of the most prestigious advertising agencies, published these revealing words in one of their publications: "The backbone of the typical advertising agency's business in the 19th Century was patent medicines ..."

The dawn of the new age of "fairness in advertising."

The Federal Trades Commission was born in 1914 at the dawn of the new age of "fairness in advertising." A famous "Sears-Roebuck confession" was published which also began to waken the suspicions of a wary public, and today, we have Nader's Raiders championing the cause and keeping halter on some of the more outlandish purveyors of "hype." But even before these early reformers, a few very wise merchants recognized the value of honesty in advertising. In the 1820's, A.T. Stewart, who was succeeded by John Wanamaker, became New York's first

THE JOHN WANAMAKER STORE

THE MEN'S STORE OPENS AT 7:30 TOMORROW (WEDNESDAY) TO USHER IN

The Greatest Sale in the History of Men's Clothing

John Wanamaker
FORMERLY A. T. STEWART & CO
8th to 10th, Broadway to Fourth Ave
Telephone 4700 Stuyvesant.

TUESDAY, JANUARY 5, 1915

Philadelphia Store, 13th to Juniper Chestnut to Market
Paris Bureau, 44 Rue des Petites Ecuries
London Bureau, 13 and 14 Pall Mall East, opposite Trafalgar Square

"To speak truly of the store and its merchandise" is the simple rule of Wanamaker publicity

The Pity of It

to be like the winter's stormy days spreading colds and dampnesses all around—

The Pity of It!

There is no raincoat to be had for money that will cure the careless and cultivated habit of pouring out the dark side and the disagreeable, and plunging everybody about you into the distemper of miserableness

It is a "pat speech" of a boy picked up from his father—"Oh, it is just my way, you must not mind me."

The monkey in the Zoo that bites the fingers of the boy who feeds him might grin and say in his own queer chatter, "It is only my way," but the boy's smarting fingers tell the suffering boy that it is a bad way

There are bad ways of storekeeping.

Some people will never learn.

The only way we have found to get the good people here is to pick them quite young, and plant the virgin soil before it has been filled with things that have to be pulled up and thrown away

But all of us here, the old and the young, are still in school studying daily lessons whereby the business must be better and better this year

The New Year starts with a good "go"

[*Signed*]

John Wanamaker

January 5
1915

The White Sale That Grows in Interest

You can come to this Wanamaker Sale of White day after day, and each time discover something you haven't seen before

Never was there a more fascinating collection of new and different lingerie than you will find here

We extend to you a most earnest invitation to come and see for yourself

Third floor Old Building

Curtains

Disposal Averaging HALF PRICE

manufacturer's entire season's surplus of 4,276 pairs of curtains is here at prices averaging half less than regular Wanamaker rates

$1, $1.50, $1.75 and $2.25 Pair

Every kind of curtain is included — marquisette scrim and net, trimmed with all kinds of laces.

Third Gallery, New Building.

Sale of Silk-and-Cotton Ratine, 28c Yard

Special purchase of 3,895 yards, 38 inches wide—all the maker had left—of this lovely fabric which is usually sold at 68c yard.

It is so finely woven, lustrous and souple that it is admirable material for afternoon, street or dancing frocks.

Colors—light blue, navy, cadet, lavender, rose, gunmetal, sand, tan, brown, together with black and white. Also some two-tone effects.

Also $3 Imported Colored Broadcloth at $1.40 Yard

54 inches wide, a superb quality and rich shades.

Dress Fabrics Salon,
First floor, Old Building.

Unusual Linens in This Sale of White

Once in the Linen Store, you are immediately impressed with two things, the vastness and the fullness of the stocks. And these are the chief features of this January Sale of Linens. Never have we had more or better linens to offer

For instance,

A special purchase of hand drawn and hand-embroidered lace, trimmed scarfs and centerpieces at the following unusual prices

Scarfs, from 18 x 36 to 18 x 72 inches are now marked $1 to $2.75, regularly $2 to $5.50

Centerpieces, 24 inches square or round, $1.25, regularly $2.50; 30-inch size, $1.50, regularly $3.

Irish Damask Tablecloths and Napkins

In a large range of new patterns.

72 x 72 inches, $3, were $4.50.
72 x 90 inches, $3.75, were $5.50.
72 x 108 inches, $4.50, were $6.75
81 x 81 inches, $4.50, were $6.75.

Napkins to match, 24 x 24 inches, $4.75 a dozen, were $6.75.

A less expensive cloth from an Irish manufacturer, 70 x 72, $2, 70 x 90, $2.50, 70 x 108, $3.

22-inch napkins to match, $3 dozen

Special Damask, $1 Yard

72-inch double satin damask, in a large range of patterns, $1, formerly $1.25. In some patterns, 24-inch napkins to match, $3.50 dozen, formerly $4.50.

Also our regular $1.50 double satin damask, 72 inches wide, for $1.20

In some patterns, 24-inch napkins to match, $3.75.

Special—Scalloped tablecloths, 2 x 2 yards, in round designs, $3.75, formerly in our own stock at $5.50.

Linen Sheets and Sheeting

90-inch pure linen bleached sheeting of unusual quality for 85c a yard.

Bleached pure linen sheets, hemstitched, 90 x 96 in. (full bed size), $4.75 a pair; 72 x 96 in. (single bed size), $4.25 a pair

Hand-drawn and hand-hemstitched linen sheets, woven of round thread linen, 72 x 96 in., $7.75 a pair, formerly $8.75; 90 x 96 in., $10 a pair, formerly $11.75.

Pillow cases to match, 22½ x 36 in., $1.85 a pair formerly $2.25.

Towels in the Sale

A special purchase of all linen huckaback towels, $3, $3.60, $4.20, $4.80, $6.

Turkish towels, extra weight, $1.50, $3.60, $4.20, $6 A special purchase

Linen Store,
First floor, Old Building

Mission Furniture at Halved Prices

Quaint mission furniture from Stickley Brothers Co. ("The Old House")

$132,321 worth, for every room in the house

$2.50 instead of $5

For a well-made rocker or dining room chair. From that price up to $24 for a $48 rocker and $25.75 for a $51.50 leather-covered library chair, there's quite a range of prices in chairs and rockers.

Settees start at $12.75

For the $25.50 kind, and grade slowly up to $51.50 for the great comfortable $103 kind

China closets

Regularly $32.50 are $16.25, and on to $63 for the $126 kind

Serving tables,

$8 to $13.50, instead of $16.25 to $27, the regular prices.

Plenty of living-room tables

Beginning at $4.50, instead of $9, and running up to $25.75 instead of $51.50.

Sideboards

are $18 to $36, instead of $36 to $72.

Extension tables,

$15.50 to $31.50, instead of $31 to $63.

Magazine and book racks, book cases, waste paper holders, tabourettes, footstools, costumers, mirrors, dinner gongs—all half usual rates, bringing them down to very little prices.

All the Stickley family

are famous as makers of good furniture and particularly of mission furniture, and not least amongst the number is the Stickley Bros. Co. of Grand Rapids.

Never before

has this great factory offered so large a lot of their goods at such an almost unheard of price.

We believe this

to be one of the most valuable furniture offerings we have ever made and the public knows how famous are our great sales in furniture.

Fifth Gallery, New Building.

The John Wanamaker Store

We don't like superlatives. They have been much misused; have lost a great deal of their dictionary meaning. But when we tried to avoid them in telling the news of this Sale we were "up a tree." We could find only one phrase to fit the facts—*the greatest sale in the history of men's clothing.*

This is the First Annual National Clearaway of Men's Better Suits and Overcoats

From the Great National Clothing Manufacturers and from Our Own Stocks

5,420 brand new suits and overcoats, just unpacked, from the leading clothing manufacturers of America, and 7,223 fancy suits and overcoats from the fine regular Wanamaker stocks—all that remain.

Ha! Ha Ha.

Everybody will be pleased—the men who made those fine suits and overcoats, we who offer them, and the men who get them and make the real savings that go with them. One of the hundreds of men who wait for the Annual Wanamaker Clearaway asked us about it the other day. We told him we had broadened it how, months ago, when the manufacturing tailors were busy on this winter's orders, we had gone to the best of them, looked over their fabrics, picked the ones we wanted and said to them—"*We'll take whatever you have left over of these fabrics when you've filled your winter orders, make them up into suits—or overcoats—the Wanamaker way, take your time about it, only get them to us the first of the year,*" how they were mightily pleased to have part of their surplus so easily provided for, and we got the terms we wanted; and how our customers were to get all the benefits. He was a most tickled man when he left, vowing to be here Wednesday morning at 7.30

12,643 Men's Suits and Overcoats

This is the largest number ever set out for sale under one roof, on one floor (the street floor), a selected stock, representative of the better clothes America has produced this season, honestly-made, serviceable fabrics, fashionably cut, a very wide choice of patterns, $355,485 worth, figured on the basis of our regular prices, to be offered for $223,337.75, a total saving of $132,147.25

(See tables below; some men will save $50.50 on one purchase each, average saving is over $10.)

There are 6,223 Suits

Young men's suits, conservative suits: hundreds of patterns more than 3,000 made from imported fabrics.

On the Burlington Arcade floor Fourth Avenue End

506 of $30	Wanamaker grade	$23.50 (2,058 Suits)
452 of $32.50	Wanamaker grade	
366 of $35	Wanamaker grade	
318 of $37.50	Wanamaker grade	
215 of $40	Wanamaker grade	
201 of $45	Wanamaker grade	
683 of $25	Wanamaker grade	$18.50 (2,067 Suits)
726 of $27.50	Wanamaker grade	
658 of $30	Wanamaker grade	

In the New Store for Men. Broadway corner Eighth

585 of $20	Wanamaker grade	$14.50 (1,215 Suits)
411 of $22.50	Wanamaker grade	
219 of $25	Wanamaker grade	
281 of $15	Wanamaker grade	$11.50 (883 Suits)
363 of $18	Wanamaker grade	
239 of $20	Wanamaker grade	

Note—This is a most astonishing group of good-patterned, well-made, serviceable suits. Some soft roll coats, some with patch pockets; the greater part cut in a medium conservative fashion.

There are 6,420 Overcoats

(4,252 have silk lining and silk sleeves 1,155 have silk lining.)

On the Burlington Arcade floor Fourth Avenue End

Black and Oxford Overcoats

460 of $35	Wanamaker grade	$24.50 (1,721 Overcoats)
408 of $40	Wanamaker grade	
352 of $45	Wanamaker grade	
207 of $48.50	Wanamaker grade	
137 of $50	Wanamaker grade	
141 of $70	Wanamaker grade	
16 of $75	Wanamaker grade	

Fancy Overcoats

203 of $27.50	Wanamaker grade	$19.50 (1,388 Overcoats)
410 of $30	Wanamaker grade	
210 of $35	Wanamaker grade	
311 of $40	Wanamaker grade	
254 of $45	Wanamaker grade	

On the Burlington Arcade floor Broadway End

All Fancy Overcoats

387 of $20	Wanamaker grade	$14.50 (1,143 Overcoats)
462 of $22.50	Wanamaker grade	
294 of $25	Wanamaker grade	
397 of $15	Wanamaker grade	$11.50 (1,155 Overcoats)
245 of $16.50	Wanamaker grade	
321 of $18	Wanamaker grade	
192 of $20	Wanamaker grade	

At Subway Entrance, New Building

257 of $12.50	Wanamaker grade	$9.75 (1,013 Overcoats)
355 of $13.50	Wanamaker grade	
401 of $15	Wanamaker grade	

Note—2,298 of these overcoats are either quarter, half or full silk-lined. Fashionable lengths and patterns: loose and Chesterfield-Wanamaker models

Men Know What to Expect of a Wanamaker Sale

And this beats them all. Detailed description is unnecessary.

There will be suits and overcoats in all sizes, for every taste

A body of our best clothing salesmen from the Philadelphia Store came over today, and with representatives of the great manufacturing houses; and picked extra salesmen, are getting acquainted with all the stocks; so that you will be intelligently and promptly waited upon tomorrow.

There will be plenty of fitting rooms, and the tailoring force has been tripled, so that alterations may proceed with despatch. There will be no charge for alterations.

Stout men will please go straight to the Burlington Arcade, south bay; tall men to the Burlington Arcade, north bay. Signs will help you to find the place.

In order to give every man a chance to buy the best suit or overcoat of his size in the sale, none will be sent out on approval, and a deposit will be required upon every C. O. D purchase.

The sale will begin at 7.30—note the earlier hour—tomorrow morning. All the doors in the New Building, and the door leading from the Astor Place Station on the Subway, will be opened at that hour

Some of the lesser-priced overcoats will be on tables by the Subway Entrance, for men who are in a special hurry.

The Men's Store will open tomorrow morning at 7:30 to give every man a chance.

More Than 100 Extra Salesmen | **No Charge for Alterations**

"Merchant-Prince" largely because of his truthful advertising. Wanamaker, incidentally, believed that "the customer is king" and was probably responsible for the phrase "the customer is always right."

Another old Wanamaker ad stated:

> We have a lot of rotten raincoats we want to get rid
> of.

They were sold out the next morning at a price the public gladly paid.   And once he advertised some dollar neckties in this way:

> they're not as good as they look, but they're good for
> 25 cents.

One of the earliest advocates of truth in advertising.

The author of many of those old ads was John E. Powers, one of the earliest advocates of truth in advertising.   A Pittsburgh department store, in financial straits, once asked his advice and soon thereafter published a large ad which read:

> We are bankrupt. We owe $125,000 more than we
> can pay, and this announcement will bring our
> creditors down on our necks. But if you come and
> <u>buy</u> tomorrow, we shall have the money to meet
> them. If not, we shall go to the wall.

This display of truth and showmanship, it is said, saved the store.

After the Civil War the St. Joseph's Oil Company grew so quickly they were able to spend $600,000 for advertising. The proprietor, C. A. Vogeler, was most enthusiastic about outdoor advertising, which then consisted mostly of barn and fence post signs. Once he even went so far as to buy a Mississippi River steamboat for delivering his remedy, but mainly because he could use it as a giant billboard. The words "St. Joseph's Oil" were so large they could be read for miles. Another time he had the oil's name conspicuously painted on a rock at Niagara Falls and only under duress removed it after he had milked as much publicity out of it as he could.

Even though the reputation of advertising men was held in low regard, advertising itself created flourishing businesses and made quite a few people wealthy. Thomas Holloway, a British pill maker, spent 5,000 pounds a year on advertising in 1842 and by 1860 his budget increased to 45,000 pounds!

Barratt would look up from his sales figures and smile.

Another Englishman, Thomas J. Barratt, became a partner in a sleepy little firm that manufactured Pears' Soap. In 1865 the firm spent 80 pounds on advertising, but within a decade they boosted their advertising outlay to 100,000 pounds a year. Pears' Soap became the most widely known commercial product in the world. When Barratt's critics wondered who read the "useless signs" Barratt would look up from his sales figures and smile. One of their ads showed a bedraggled old tramp who was quoted as saying: "Two years ago I used your soap. Since then, I have used no other."

The following pages feature two very old Pears' Soap ads.

So actual cash payments were an incentive.

In 1865 a fellow named George P. Rowell resigned his position with the *Boston Post* to start his own advertising agency. Rowell enterprisingly established a service with a list of 100 newspapers quoting realistic circulation estimates and assured his clients their money would be wisely used if they advertised on the "Rowell List." The majority of the papers gave him as much as 75% discount and he promised them continued patronage as well as cash payments. In those days payment for services rendered was usually paid with eggs, poultry, vegetables, etc. So actual cash payments were an incentive. Rowell also bought newspaper space in bulk and retailed it. Since the patent medicine business was quite lucrative, Rowell decided he would take advantage of it and had a medical student from a New York hospital "brew up something useful." The young man decided on a "liquid having a soothing effect on the stomach." Rowell's ad copy claimed:

· How Very Comfortable !

This is the sort of feeling that you have after a bath or a wash with Pears—a feeling of natural freshness—the exhilaration due to a sense of perfect cleanliness—the glow and delight of a healthy stimulating influence.

Pears is composed entirely of natural saponaceous ingredients of the highest emollient and detergent properties. It is so daintily soothing and softening to the skin surface, and it promotes in a pre-eminent degree that natural beauty of complexion which is universally admired.

Pears' Soap

Best aid to the Health and Beauty of the Skin

Matchless for the Complexion

Pears is the *Most Economical of Toilet Soaps* because of its Double-Lasting Qualities

OF ALL SCENTED SOAPS PEARS' OTTO OF ROSE IS THE BEST

1891

PEARS' SOAP.

IT IS MATCHLESS FOR THE COMPLEXION.

SOLE GOLD MEDALS FOR TOILET SOAP.—PARIS.

"OUR BABY."

From the original picture by The Honorable John COLLIER.
The property of the Proprietors of PEARS' Soap.

☞ Insist on having **PEARS' Soap.** Substitutes are sometimes recommended by druggists and shopkeepers for the sole purpose of making more profit out of you.

No matter what ails a man, it is either as a result of stomach difficulty or it will, to some extent, induce such a difficulty.

The liquid, however, was far from pleasing to the eye and tasted as bad, so rather than abandon the project, the medication was made in pill form and eventually became a very profitable business.

You must write your advertisements to catch damned fools--not college professors.

In writing advertisements for the medicine, Rowell heeded the advice of an experienced medicine man: "You must write your advertisements to catch damned fools -- not college professors. Then you'll catch as many college professors as you will any other sort."

The patent medicine era brought on the showman-type advertising man, loud, eloquent and given to great hyperbole and enclosed in the parenthesis of blaring bugles or rolling drums or twanging banjo music. P.T. Barnum was probably the grand-daddy of them all. Here's an ad for liniment written by Barnum:

APPRECIATED

ALAS, poor Jumbo! But Messrs. Barnum, Baily and Hutchinson are still the owners of over fifty Elephants. In their travels we have reason to believe that all these intelligent beasts carry CENTAUR LINIMENT in their trunks.

This is what Barnum Says

438 Fifth Avenue, New York, May 9, 1875

Among my vast troop of teamsters, equestrians, horses, camels and elephants, there are always some lame, wounded, galled and strained. My doctors and veterinaries all assure me that nothing has proven so prompt and efficacious a remedy for men and animals as CENTAUR LINIMENT. If you could supply me with a live Centaur, I will give you a check for $100,000.

An 1891 patent medicine ad is featured on the next page.

1891

"Twin roses by the zephyr blown apart,
Only to meet again more close, and share
The inward fragrance of each other's heart."

So Keats describes the lovers in "Isabella." Many lovers have been separated because the health of the lady in the case failed. No man finds attraction in a woman who is subject to nervous excitability, exhaustion, prostration, hysteria, spasms and other distressing, nervous symptoms, commonly attendant upon functional derangement and organic diseases peculiar to women.

The remedy for all such maladies is Dr. Pierce's Favorite Prescription. As a soothing and strengthening nervine it is unequaled. As an invigorating tonic, it imparts strength to the uterine organs as well as to the whole system. Contains no alcohol to inebriate ; no sugar or syrup to derange digestion ; a legitimate *medicine*, not a *beverage*.

For all displacements, as prolapsus, retroversion, anteversion and flexions, causing weak and aching back, bearing-down sensations, ulceration, unnatural discharges and kindred ailments, the "Favorite Prescription" is an unequaled remedy, and the *only guaranteed* one.

You only pay for *the good* you get in using Dr. Pierce's Favorite Prescription.

Can you ask more?

World's Dispensary Medical Association, Proprietors, Buffalo, N. Y.

By 1880 Lydia E. Pinkham's small "family kitchen" enterprise was becoming successful, so Lydia decided to put into advertising every cent that could be spared. Not only was she a good business woman but she also had a flair for copywriting:

> A sure cure for Prolapsus Uteri, or Falling of the Womb ... a great help in pregnancy, it relieves pain during labor ... second to no remedy that has ever been before the public.

One of Lydia's ads is featured next page.

Her ads were directed at lonely and anxious women and made each feel she was talking to her alone. So powerful were these ads that no Pinkham would ever be in need.

When Lydia Pinkham died in 1883 the family was very fortunate to find James T. Wetheral, a Boston advertising man, who could write ads that sounded sympathetic and in a "just us girls" way, almost as if dictated by Lydia, herself.

As late as 1905 the Sears-Roebuck Catalog contained 20 pages of small type to advertise scores of patent medicines including drugs guaranteed to cure all manner of ills. Among them, blood purifiers, laxatives, liver and kidney remedies, pile remedies, worm-killers, fat reducers, stomach pills, and "Injection Number Seven", described as a "cure for gonorrhea in one to five days" as well as its own "White Star Liquor Cure" which a wife could put in her husband's food or drink without his knowledge. Not until 1913 did Sear's policy pertaining to patent medicines change. In their catalog of that date, on page 670, appeared a statement to the effect that because dangerous drugs were likely to cause harm to anyone who took them, Sears would offer only those drugs listed in the U.S. Pharmacopedia, or the national formulary, or which were approved by the American Medical Association. The announcement concluded by saying:

If any of our customers have need for more than a few simple home remedies ... we are frankly of the opinion that they should consult their family physician rather than waste their time and money experimenting with drugs, whether patent medicine or any other.

It sold products by the ton.

The patent medicine businessmen soon discovered that good testimonials were almost priceless, especially the before-and-after variety. It gave the prospective customer confidence and faith when reading an independent confirmation, and it sold products by the ton.

When the Pure Food & Drug Act was passed in 1906 several patent medicine manufactures continued misrepresenting their products, but after it was seen that enforcement by jail or heavy fines was the order of the day, patent medicines disappeared almost entirely.

From that humble beginning the advertising industry and agency business grew together.

According to the *Britannica*, the very first agency was opened in Philadelphia by Volney B. Palmer in 1840. In the beginning, he had to supplement his income by selling real estate, coal and firewood. From that humble beginning the advertising industry and the agency business grew together and had everything to do with the marketing of goods and services as we know it today. As agencies prospered, they attracted the nubile minds of each generation whose ingenuity, wit and cleverness refined selling techniques and revolutionized the free enterprise system. Entrepreneurs were less and less inclined to start a business simply because they had a bright idea for a new product or a service, and more because they had figured a way to fill a new "need" and a way to reach buyers who would pay money to have that need filled. Where the need was not patently obvious, the medium of advertising created the need in the minds of the masses, and then proceeded to tell them how they could gain fulfillment, for a price.

The first agency to represent the buyer rather than the seller of advertising space was N.W. Ayer & Company, established in Philadelphia in 1869. It used the "agency compensation system" still used today. One of their ads dated 1899 is featured next page.

This may have been the most fortunate mistake in the annuls of advertising.

This next may have been the most fortunate mistake in the annuls of advertising. The proprietor of *New York Ledger*, a weekly family paper of fiction and morality articles, was a man named Robert Bonner. Circulation was shaky, so Bonner decided to try a small ad in the pages of a large competitor, the *New York Herald*, then very well established. He composed an eight word announcement:

Read Mrs. Southworth's New Story in the Ledger..

"The larger the advertising message, the more you will sell."

He then sent it to the *Herald* for publication. In almost illegible handwriting, along the border, he scrawled "one line." The *Herald* composer, misread the mechanical direction line, thinking it to say "one page." The line was repeated in that day's edition, covering a full page. When Bonner saw the paper he nearly had apoplexy, for he did not have enough money in the bank to begin to pay for such an ad. By mid-afternoon, however, the entire issue of the Ledger had been sold, as well as a second printing. After that, no man was ever able to convince Robert Bonner that advertising does not pay. He became a staunch supporter of the other philosophy: "The larger the advertising message, the more you will sell."

It became the catch phrases for P&G's most popular soap.

Another accidental bonanza, this at Proctor & Gamble in the early days, resulted through an error in an experimental batch of soap which occurred in 1878. The soap came out white because someone neglected to put in the expensive olive oil. And it floated because a workman forgot to shut off the beaters when he left for lunch, resulting in more air being whipped into the mixture. Rather than take a loss on that particular batch, the Proctor & Gamble marketers decided to call it their "white soap", and claim it as one of their 24 varieties. But after receiving several orders for "that soap that floats", Mr. Proctor realized this soap to have special sales possibilities. He sent samples to a testing laboratory.

Old Prob. Senior

1899

There is an older old probability than the Signal Service Chief. The original is a twin of human life.

Probability pervades all business affairs. To reckon with it well is to succeed; to ignore it is to fail; to wait till it is entirely eliminated is not to start.

In Newspaper Advertising the element of probability is naturally a specially interesting factor. In this line it is like the sweet potato in Aunt Dinah's famous pies—the less of that the better.

The best forecasters as to probability are observation and experience. These are what the Weather Bureau works with, and these are what we place at the service of Newspaper and Magazine Advertisers.

If any one is interested in the probability of such a plan in such papers producing such a result with such an outlay, he might find a good answer in our wide experience of thirty years. It's wise to be as wise as possible before the event.

An inquiry need cost nothing. If you are interested in Newspaper Advertising, we are interested in you.

N. W. AYER & SON,
PHILADELPHIA.

NEWSPAPER ADVERTISING.

MAGAZINE ADVERTISING.

I've included four Ivory ads on the following pages.

He dreamed up the slogan "shot from guns".

The report stated that White Soap was 99 and 44/100ths percent pure. ("Pure" what was not specified.) All that was needed was a catchy name and he got his inspiration for that at church one Sunday morning in 1879. The minister was reading from the 45th Psalm: "All thy garments smell of myrrh, and aloes, and cassia, out of the ivory palaces, whereby they have made thee glad." "IVORY -- IT FLOATS -- 99 and 44/100ths percent pure" became the catch phrases for P&G's most popular soap, and now you know the rest of the story.

"ABSOLUTELY PURE" was the slogan of the Royal Baking Powder Company and it helped bring their sales into the millions. The impact of slogans brought about interesting incidents such as the often repeated story of one famous ad campaign. The print ad showed a little girl, kneeling at her bedside, praying: "Bless Mommy and Daddy and Baby Bruvver, and make me absolutely pure like Royal Baking Powder -- not just 99-44/100ths percent pure, like Ivory Soap."

Quaker Oats' "Puff Berries" and "Wheat Berries" ads showed Orientals eating rice -- and some believed this ethnic slant was the reason sales were slumping at Quaker. The company brought in the famous and legendary Claude Hopkins to do some repair work on their ad campaign. The Chicago advertising man recommended the cereals be given a new set of names -- "Puffed Wheat" and "Puffed Rice", and also that they should be higher priced. He dreamed up the slogan "shot from guns" and centered the ads around that and the process inventor, Prof. A.P. Anderson. Not long after, sales skyrocketed, and the company started "smiling all the way to the bank" once again.

I've included one of those famous "shot from guns" ads on page 214.

Most girls have some dainty belongings that they delight in caring for themselves, and by this careful attention they preserve the beauty of their pretty things and avoid the destructive tendencies of a careless laundress.

The main thing needed in washing delicate fabrics is a perfectly safe soap. Ivory Soap has been shown by the most critical tests to be made of only pure materials. Ivory Soap is effective, yet so mild that it is safe to use on anything that water will not injure.

1899

THE "IVORY" is a Laundry Soap, with all the fine qualities of a choice Toilet Soap, and is 99 44-100 **per cent. pure.**

Ladies will find this Soap especially adapted for washing laces, infants' clothing, silk hose, cleaning gloves and all articles of fine texture and delicate color, and for the varied uses about the house that daily arise, requiring the use of soap that is above the ordinary in quality.

For the Bath, Toilet, or Nursery it is preferred to most of the Soaps sold for toilet use, being purer and much more pleasant and effective and possessing all the desirable properties of the finest unadultered White Castile Soap. The Ivory Soap will " **float.**"

The cakes are so shaped that they may be used **entire** for general purposes or divided with a **stout** thread (as illustrated) into two perfectly **formed cakes,** of convenient size for toilet use.

The **price,** compared to the quality and the size of the cakes, makes it the cheapest Soap for everybody for every want. TRY IT.

SOLD EVERYWHERE.

Advertising Men

REACH FOR THE FLOATER*
INSTEAD

"**A**DVERTISING men would *walk miles* for the Bath-Soap-That-Floats." "Advertising men *reach for a floater instead of a sinker.*"

Even our best friends told us this! But we wanted to be sure.

We wrote the 549 advertising managers of America's 549 largest companies. We asked them, "What bath soap do you prefer?" And they rolled up more votes for Ivory than for any other!

Advertising men vote for Ivory—simply because that's the way most men feel about bath soaps.

Most men don't want to strain their muscles or impair their good humor with deep sea diving after sinker soaps.

Most men don't want to smell like the flowers of spring either!

Most men (and most wives might as well know it) warble more cheerfully, relax more completely, in the clean-smelling foam of an Ivory bath—with a big, man-sized cake of Ivory, floating in easy reach.

*IVORY SOAP

99⁴⁴/₁₀₀% Pure · It floats

KIND TO EVERYTHING IT TOUCHES

A girl can't be *too* careful

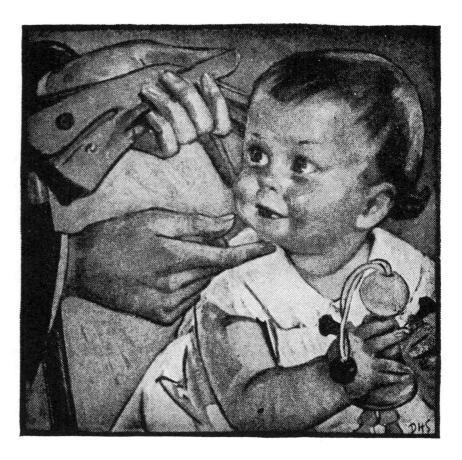

Now that I'm ten months old, I've decided that a girl can't start too young with the *right* beauty treatment.

Why, some gentlemen of my acquaintance have barked like dogs and walked like bears for the privilege of kissing my cheek. And grown-up ladies are really envious of my complexion.

But I'm not conceited. After all, it was the nice doctor at the hospital who suggested the very best beauty treatment for my very sensitive skin. When Mother asked him, he said, "Why not use Ivory? You can't find a purer, milder soap."

In fairness to him, I always mention this fact when I give my exclusive beauty talks in my Ivory bath.

But I haven't told you about Mother yet. *Now she's using my cake of Ivory.* Of course,

it's perfectly all right, as she's always been very nice to me. In fact, I'm glad. She's so pretty that she deserves to use the finest soap!

But one thing is a mystery to me—what Father said to her. "Where are all those fussy lotions and creams you used to have around?" he asked with a smile.

"Don't be silly!" Mother said. I thought she acted a little confused.

Now Mother is going to be prettier still, since she's taking a beauty course with Ivory!

An Ivory Baby · Her Mark

·· however grown-up she may be!

P S. Your complexion is a baby's complexion that has grown up. A bit less silky. A trifle less sensitive. But even more than a baby's your complexion needs Ivory's beauty help. For the skin can create its own fresh beauty. But it cannot clean itself. And its clear fresh tone will be dulled if the pores are clogged by dust and make-up.

There are no "if's" and "but's" about cleanliness. Soap and water are the best cleansers. And you'll find that Ivory cleansing will "wake up" your complexion so pleasantly. For Ivory is perfectly pure. Can your complexion afford to use a less gentle and safe soap than Ivory—which cherishes the delicate beauty of millions of babies?

PROCTER & GAMBLE

IVORY SOAP *Kind to everything it touches—99 $\frac{44}{100}$% pure—it floats*

SUNDAY Is Puffed Grain Day

Why So?

In a million homes Sunday seems to be the chief day for Puffed Wheat and Puffed Rice. So all of our evidence indicates.

Can you understand why that is so?

That is partly due to Sunday suppers—these bubble-like grains in milk. Then a great many people think of Puffed Grains as dainties, too good for every day.

That's a Great Mistake

Of course, Puffed Grains are dainties. They are light and airy, thin and flaky, with a fascinating taste. They are the food confections. But they are also more than that.

Puffed Wheat and Puffed Rice are whole-grain foods, with the grains puffed to eight times normal size.

They are scientific foods, invented by Prof. A. P. Anderson—a famous dietitian.

They are the only grain foods so prepared that every food cell is exploded. Digestion is made easy and complete, so that every atom feeds.

It's a great mistake to serve such foods infrequently. There are three kinds, so you get a variety. They make the ideal breakfast dish. Mixed with fruit, they form a delightful blend. In bowls of milk they are flavory, toasted bubbles, four times as porous as bread.

Salted or buttered, like peanuts or popcorn, they are perfect between-meal tidbits. In candy-making they are better than nut meats. They are flaky, toasted wafers for soups.

They are all-hour foods which never tax the stomach.

Puffed Wheat — Puffed Rice and Corn Puffs
Each 15c Except in Far West

We seal the grains in huge guns; then roll them for an hour in 550 degrees of heat. That gives the nut-like flavor. All the inner moisture is changed to steam; then the guns are shot. A hundred million steam explosions occur in every kernel. Every food cell is exploded, so digestion can instantly act. That is why these Puffed Grains are such airy, flimsy bubbles. Keep all three kinds on hand.

In the early 1890's jingle ads became the craze and Proctor & Gamble helped it along with their jingle contests. The initial jingles were usually one-shot efforts, mainly to amuse:

"Is there anything nearer or dearer to you than I am?"
Asked the lover with tremulous dread; "there's nothing that's dearer, but something that's nearer --
And that's my P.D. Corset", she said.

"Pin-up girl" Phoebe Snow swept the country with its appeal.

The jingles for the Lackawanna Railroad's "pin-up girl", Phoebe Snow, swept the country with its appeal. In their effort to convince the public of the cleanliness of the anthracite coal used in their engines, the jingles depicted Phoebe Snow as a very attractive young lady, impeccably dressed.

Says Phoebe Snow
About to go
Upon a trip
To Buffalo
"My gown stays white
Both day and night
Upon the Road of Anthracite."

Phoebe attracted thousands of adoring fans who avidly watched for each new episode to appear in print. Eventually she (fictitiously) met a handsome man, also dressed in white, on the train, and ultimately the two were married by a bishop, also clad in white, who also just happened to be on the same train to Buffalo. It may have been these advertising campaigners who first fostered the idea for soap operas.

Two Lackawanna Railroad ads starring the one and only Phoebe Snow are found on the following pages.

BUTTON DESIGNED AND WORN BY LACKAWANNA EMPLOYEES

Says Phoebe Snow:
"These emblems show
Your pride in letting
People know
That day or night
Their safety's quite
First rule on Road
    of Anthracite."

Safety means efficiency. Personal efficiency minimizes accidents. That's why Lackawanna employees are striving to put "Safety First" above every other consideration. The button which they have adopted is intended to fasten the grip of safety on every mile of Lackawanna track.

Lackawanna Railroad

The Road of Anthracite

Yes, Phoebe, I
Can now see why
The praises of
This road you cry:
My gloves are white
As when last night
We took the Road
Of Anthracite.

Lackawanna Railroad

It was due to the discovery that nothing could sell a product or service faster than the skillful use of emotional appeals.

Advertising knowledge and approach experienced a gigantic growth proliferation in the first decade of the Twentieth Century. It was due to the discovery that nothing could sell a product or service faster than the skillful use of emotional appeals. Theodore F. MacManus, originally from Buffalo, gave up a city editor's position in Toledo to try his hand at writing advertising copy for Detroit's new automobile industry. It was a wise move on his part for he became so expert in the field his name was revered throughout the industry for forty years. The most famous of his ads, headlined -- "The Penalty of Leadership" was for the Cadillac Company, and first appeared in the January 2, 1915 issue of The *Saturday Evening Post*. Its snobbishly dignified message indicated that Cadillac ownership overcame all personality problems because it was incomparably superior to all other autos. This ad struck such a responsive chord that Cadillac has been filling requests for reprints ever since.

MacManus' ads made him a millionaire and he seemed to take much pleasure in non-participation. Once he even had a private golf course built on his estate, but never learned to play the game. Occasionally he walked around the course for exercise and, in the words of James Playsted Wood, "to dispel his dislike of advertising ... too much of which he concluded, was cheap, blatant and tricky."

They ushered in a kind of copywriting that spread far beyond autos.

Automobile ads changed about 1915 when advertising concentrated on smart and elegant styling, rather than the mechanical excellence and the joys of the open road. This type of advertising marked the beginning of the stylist era and was used in advertising everything from autos to power boats, rotary can openers and most any other mechanical device. Ad headlines "Somewhere West of Laramie" and "The Penalty of Leadership" are usually hailed as the greatest auto ads ever run. They ushered in a kind of copywriting that spread far beyond autos and became a valuable tool for the sale of fashionable clothes, resorts, liquors, furs, jewelry and perfumes. "Word magic" is one term used for this type copy.

The PENALTY OF LEADERSHIP

IN every field of human endeavor, he that is first must perpetually live in the white light of publicity. ¶Whether the leadership be vested in a man or in a manufactured product, emulation and envy are ever at work. ¶In art, in literature, in music, in industry, the reward and the punishment are always the same. ¶The reward is widespread recognition; the punishment, fierce denial and detraction. ¶When a man's work becomes a standard for the whole world, it also becomes a target for the shafts of the envious few. ¶If his work be merely mediocre, he will be left severely alone—if he achieve a masterpiece, it will set a million tongues a-wagging. ¶Jealousy does not protrude its forked tongue at the artist who produces a commonplace painting. ¶Whatsoever you write, or paint, or play, or sing, or build, no one will strive to surpass, or to slander you, unless your work be stamped with the seal of genius. ¶Long, long after a great work or a good work has been done, those who are disappointed or envious continue to cry out that it can not be done. ¶Spiteful little voices in the domain of art were raised against our own Whistler as a mountebank, long after the big world had acclaimed him its greatest artistic genius. ¶Multitudes flocked to Bayreuth to worship at the musical shrine of Wagner, while the little group of those whom he had dethroned and displaced argued angrily that he was no musician at all. ¶The little world continued to protest that Fulton could never build a steamboat, while the big world flocked to the river banks to see his boat steam by. ¶The leader is assailed because he is a leader, and the effort to equal him is merely added proof of that leadership. ¶Failing to equal or to excel, the follower seeks to depreciate and to destroy—but only confirms once more the superiority of that which he strives to supplant. ¶There is nothing new in this. ¶It is as old as the world and as old as the human passions—envy, fear, greed, ambition, and the desire to surpass. ¶And it all avails nothing. ¶If the leader truly leads, he remains—the leader. ¶Master-poet, master-painter, master-workman, each in his turn is assailed, and each holds his laurels through the ages. ¶That which is good or great makes itself known, no matter how loud the clamor of denial. ¶That which deserves to live—lives.

Somewhere West of Laramie

SOMEWHERE west of Laramie there's a broncho-busting, steer-roping girl who knows what I'm talking about. She can tell what a sassy pony, that's a cross between greased lightning and the place where it hits, can do with eleven hundred pounds of steel and action when he's going high, wide and handsome.

The truth is—the Playboy was built for her.

Built for the lass whose face is brown with the sun when the day is done of revel and romp and race.

She loves the cross of the wild and the tame.

There's a savor of links about that car—of laughter and lilt and light—a hint of old loves—and saddle and quirt. It's a brawny thing—yet a graceful thing for the sweep o' the Avenue.

Step into the Playboy when the hour grows dull with things gone dead and stale.

Then start for the land of real living with the spirit of the lass who rides, lean and rangy, into the red horizon of a Wyoming twilight.

JORDAN MOTOR CAR COMPANY, Inc., Cleveland, Ohio

Mail order advertising really came of age in the early 20's although it had been born long before that. Richard W. Sears demonstrated the feasibility of selling by mail with his catalog of watches and its success developed into the mammoth Sears, Roebuck & Company.

In the 1880's some firms had already invented "keys" that were indicated in the address or box number, drawer or department. This helped identify the source of the ad and permitted comparing of effectiveness of the different ads.

Before the turn of the century, Ralph Tilton, a picturesque early ad man, invented the idea of a coupon with the ad to help stimulate immediate action. A person had to fill in his name, address and name of magazine or paper where the ad was found.

One of the greatest commodities to sell by mail proved to be books. It also helped launch other profitable businesses.

One of the greatest commodities to sell by mail proved to be books. It was a gradual process but once it caught on it also helped launch other profitable businesses such as correspondence schools, body building courses, memory improvement courses, etc.

Advertising, basically has not changed much over the centuries. It is interesting to note the similarity. The purpose and appeals are the same today as more than 2000 years ago. It is still merely a vehicle to sway people toward the forces that influence their lives, and decision-making through public persuasiveness.

Advertising admittedly has been misused and abused, and so long as man continues to have moral flaws in his nature, it will no doubt continue to be. But so have man's other great inventions and discoveries -- the wheel, fire, electricity and the splitting of the atom. Advertising is one of the great "forces" equal to any of these, and will no doubt play as important a part as the others in the unfolding of our little universe here on Planet Earth.

We must elect to never "throw out the baby with the bathwater."

If some advertising sometimes seems a little foolish, the same can be said for some marriages. If it is sometimes untruthful, the same can be said of some of our prominent governmental leaders, testifying under oath. We must elect to never "throw out the baby with the bathwater," When we judge the positive and negative aspects of advertising. Fire, used intelligently, can keep us warm, cozy and comfortable. Used carelessly, it can burn our house down. The analogy is clear. Advertising claims the right to be measured by its best -- not its worst. By its successes, not its failures. Used in good conscience and responsibility, it can be the savior of the world. Used irresponsibly, it assumes another name -- propaganda. Both are forms of mass communication, and both have their uses in the universal scheme of things - both positive and negative. As Shakespeare said: "The fault, dear Brutus is not in our stars, but in us that we are underlings".

Index

A

WHO AND WHAT IS TOWERS CLUB, USA?

The Original Writer's Entrepreneurial Research Service.

That's what the acronym in our name stands for. We've been publishing a newsletter for the marketing and advertising world since February 1974. Our main theme is information merchandising, hence the name **INFO MARKETING REPORT.** For free details call Jerry or David at **1 (800) 524-4045.**

On the reverse side of this page is a coupon you may use to obtain our "thank you" gift for buying Max's last book. It's a rare collector's item. An audio tape of Max and two of his friends in advertising. What's even better, it's **FREE** to you, as a purchaser of this book, -- and a **RARE** prize!

New York City is the mecca for the giant trade publishers. But in the last 20 years, there have been a great many smaller publishing companies spring up in smaller towns and cities. Firms like TEN SPEED PRESS of Berkeley, CA., PARA PUBLISHING of Santa Barbara, CA., Jay Frederick Editions of Fairfield, IA., and many dozens of newsletters published by one and two person staffs out of their in-home offices. Many thousands of these are the result of a proliferation of activity in the borning of the INFORMATION AGE.

We at TOWERS CLub Press, Inc. are one of that "many". The year 1995 saw us enter our twenty-first year of publishing activities serving, primarily, the world of information merchandising.

We would like to fill you in on what we do here, and how we might be able to serve you in the market place. If you would care to drop us a short note telling what market your company serves, and what products or services you provide, it might be of interest to the readers of our monthly **INFO MARKETING REPORT**.

Jerry Buchanan, President,
David A. Reecher, Vice President,
TOWERS Club Press, Inc.
9107 N.W. Eleventh Ave.
Vancouver, WA 98665-6801
(P.O. Box 2038, Vancouver WA 98668)

The TOWERS Club USA
Info Marketing
Report

Formerly the TOWERS Club, USA Newsletter.
The original source of money-making news for
Information marketers the world over (since February 1974).

ISSN:1070-3179

HERE'S A LITTLE SOMETHING EXTRA FOR THOSE WHO BOUGHT THIS MAX SACKHEIM BOOK - -

Back on April 5th 1973, the Direct Marketing Association held one of its most remembered seminars. That day they had assembled three of the most respected advertising men of the 20th Century to speak to the large audience of professional ad men and women. The three were John Caples, David Altman, and Max Sackheim. Together, they filled one 60-minute audio tape with the most fascinating talks imaginable. Their chosen topic was *"The Changing Market -- or is it?"* Each delivers timeless advice just as applicable today as it was then!

We have managed to secure a rare copy of that one hour tape. It was one of the last times John Caples or Max Sackheim ever spoke before an audience of professional advertising persons. Their combined warmth, wit and wisdom rings through in every word. We'd like to send you a **FREE COPY** of this rare collector's item (if it wasn't included in your original purchase). Just fill in the below card, scissor it out and place it in an envelope addressed to: TOWERS Club Press, P.O. Box 2038, Vancouver, WA 98668. Please include three First Class U.S. Postage Stamps to cover S&H. We'll get your **free** tape on its way to you immediately. (Retail value: $19.95)